RETHINKING EQUITY

Creating a Great School for All

Edited by Stephen Murgatroyd, PhD FRSA FBPsS and
J-C Couture, PhD

Stephen Murgatroyd, PhD FRSA FBPsS
J-C Couture, PhD

Rethinking Equity – Creating a Great School for All

ISBN: 978-1-304-27866-1

Contents

Contributors

Ernest C. Clintberg

Following 25 years as a teacher and administrator, Ernie served 11 years with the Alberta Teachers' Association including appointment as Associate Executive Secretary. His EdD (2005) in educational policy studies included a focus on educational fiscal policy and equity. Ernie continues to consult and work in the field and is an Adjunct Professor of the Faculty of Education, University of Alberta.

J-C Couture

Associate Coordinator, Research the Alberta Teachers' Association. After 20 years as a classroom teacher, he completed his PhD focusing on psychoanalytic theory and its implications for understanding teacher identity and educational development. He is currently engaged in the Association's strategic planning and collaboration with international partners.

Chris Gilham

Chris Gilham is an assistant professor at St. Francis Xavier University in Nova Scotia. He teaches primarily in the Bachelor of Education program. He completed his PhD at the University of Calgary in the summer of 2013. Chris was a public school teacher for 10 years and consultant for the past six years. His current teaching and academic work involves exploring the predominant discourses surrounding children and youth assigned with emotional and behavioural disabilities and inclusion.

Stephen Murgatroyd

CEO of the Collaborative Media Group and experienced teacher, consultant and writer. He has authored over 40 books and over 300 papers in journals and magazines. He has worked extensively in Europe, North America and Asia. He lives and works in Alberta and has been a consultant for the ATA for over 30 years.

Markku Jahnukainen

Professor and Director of Special Teacher Education at the Department of Teacher Education in University of Helsinki, Finland. He is also Adjunct Professor at the University of Alberta and Fritz Karsen Visiting Research Chair in Comparative and International Inclusive and Special Education Research in Humboldt University Berlin, Germany. His research is focusing on the education policy of inclusive and special education in comparative settings. His ultimate goal is to get a holistic and really comparative picture of the history and development of the schooling using a multidisciplinary approach.

Kathy Olmstead
Currently an Associate Superintendent with Livingstone Range School Division in Alberta and also a PhD student with Queen's University in Ontario. Her 30 plus years of experiences in teaching and school administration in varied K-12 settings, jurisdictional administration, and university studies have all focused on the local, collaborative design of inclusive learning environments for every student that comes in the doors of our public schools.

W. James Paul
Jim Paul was a high school teacher for 10 years and for the past 25 a professor in the Faculty of Education, University of Calgary. Dr. Paul's academic-scholarly work features attempts at understanding and applying historical and contemporary local and international curriculum and instruction theories and practices through a variety of lenses. He is currently engaged in exploring curriculum developments with a focus on the complex tensions between globalization and internationalization.

W. John Williamson
John Williamson has been teaching for 17 years and for 15 years has specialized in working with diverse learners in high school settings. He is also a PhD candidate in Interpretive Studies in Education at the University of Calgary pursuing an inquiry related to educational labeling and inclusion.

Pasi Sahlberg
Director General of CIMO (Centre for International Mobility and Cooperation) in Helsinki, Finland. Pasi is an international speaker and writer. Pasi is a member of the Board of Directors of ASCD (Association for Supervision and Curriculum Development) and IASCE (International Association for the Study of Cooperation in education). His book "Finnish Lessons: What can the world learn from educational change in Finland?" (2011) won the 2013 Grawemeyer Award, and he received the 2012 Education Award in Finland and 2011 Upton Sinclair Award in the United States.

Preface

A More Equitable School System – Lessons from Finland
Pasi Sahlberg, PhD

Director General of CIMO (Centre for International Mobility and Cooperation), Helsinki, Finland

Un-Finnished Business

Understanding the educational success of Alberta or Finland needs to include an awareness of socio-cultural, political, and economic factors – issues covered in several chapters of this book (see especially Chapters 1 and 3). Indeed, education policies that drive better equity and equality in these systems must be kept at the center of attention when considering any lessons from these high-performing school systems. It is difficult to imagine how Finland's educational success could be achieved or maintained without reference to the country's broader and commonly accepted system of distinctive social values that more inequitable societies may find it difficult to accept. Foreign visitors examining Finland's education system regularly conclude that the Finnish approaches to equitable schooling rely on multiple and reinforcing forms of intervention with support that teachers can get from others, in other words, strong social capital among Finland's education community.

Furthermore, Finland has shown, just like Alberta, in its own way, that educational change should be systematic and coherent, in contrast with the current haphazard intervention efforts of many other countries. My own conclusion from my life-long career as a Finnish educator and much shorter experience with Alberta's education system is that developing the capacities of schools through interventions like AISI (Alberta Initiative for School Improvement) and school-led curriculum development is much more helpful than aggressively testing students, and that some out-of-school policies for families and children associated with health, well-being and happiness are crucial.

Importing a specific aspect of Alberta's or Finland's education system, whether it is curricula, teacher training, special education, or school leadership, is probably of little value to those aiming to improve their own education systems. The Finnish welfare system guarantees all children the safety, health, nutrition, and moral support that they need to learn well in school. This is the primary lesson for more equitable schooling. Canadians understand that this is important. Keeping our school systems equitable and equal requires that these conditions exist in all schools, for all children, all the time – which is the key argument of J-C Couture's introduction to this book and that of Chapter 1.

The Finnish Way

Education policies behind Finnish reforms since the 1970s have focused on creating equal opportunities, raising quality, and increasing participation within all educational levels across Finnish society. As a result, more than 99% of the age cohort successfully completes compulsory nine-year Basic School and 95% continue their education right away in upper-secondary schools. Of those, starting upper-secondary education before, 93% eventually graduate, and are thereby eligible to attend tuition fee free higher education. Public policy is focused on the idea that equity is the driver of excellence. Contrast this with the description of Alberta's journey in Chapter 2.

Central to this effort to create equal opportunities are the principles of education and care that are typical of Finnish schools today. For example, schools are encouraged to maintain strong support systems for teaching and learning—nutritious free school meals for all pupils, health services, psychological counseling, and student guidance are normal practices in every school. Another strong element of the education system in Finland is built-in networks of schools and communities of teachers in municipalities and their seamless connection to other social services in society.

Unlike many other contemporary systems of education, the Finnish system has not been infected by market-based competition and high-stakes testing policies, often termed GERM (Global Educational Reform Movement). The main reason is that the education community in Finland has remained unconvinced that competition and choice with census-based standardized testing would be good for schools. We all know from the OECD data that the ultimate success of a high-stakes testing policy must be whether it positively affects student learning, not whether it increases student scores on a particular test. If student learning remains unaffected or gets worse, or if testing leads to biased teaching and narrower curriculum, the validity of such high-stakes tests must be questioned. Finnish education authorities and especially teachers have not been convinced that frequent external standardized testing and stronger accountability would be beneficial to students and their learning. The Finnish Way is paved with elements of equity.

Education policies are necessarily intertwined with other social policies and with the overall political culture of a nation. The key success factor in Finland's development of a well-performing, innovation-led economy with good governance and a trusted education system has been its ability to reach broad consensus on most major issues concerning future directions for Finland as a nation. Finland seems particularly successful in implementing and maintaining the policies and practices that constitute equity and equality as the basic foundation of schooling. In other words, education in Finland is seen as a public good and therefore has a strong nation-building function.

There is one more aspect of Finland's education system that is worth noting for the readers of this book that describes Alberta's journey to excellence and equity in education and its struggles with this journey. Education policies designed to raise student achievement in Finland have put a strong accent on teaching and learning by encouraging schools to craft optimal learning environments and establish instructional content that will best help students to reach the general goals of schooling. It was assumed very early in Finland's reform process that instruction is the key element that makes a difference in what students learn in school, not standards, assessment, or alternative instructional programs. As the level of teacher professionalism gradually increased in schools during the 1980s and the 1990s, the prevalence of effective teaching methods and pedagogically focused school designs increased. A new flexibility within the Finnish education system enabled schools to learn from one another, and thus make best practices universal by adopting innovative approaches to organize schooling. It also encouraged teachers and schools to continue to expand their repertoires of teaching methods and to individualize teaching in order to meet the needs of all students.

Despite the cultural and economic differences between Alberta and Finland, their school systems have notable similarities (see the exploration of this in Chapter 4). Alberta's education system today offers a compelling model because of its high quality and equitable student learning similar to the Finnish school system. One of the most significant conclusions from the OECD PISA data is that the highest-performing education systems across the OECD countries are those that combine quality with equity in education. This means that Finland, Canada, Japan, and South Korea have high average learning achievement in reading, mathematics and science with relatively weak impact from students' family background. Since there is natural socio-economic diversity in both Alberta and Finland among their students, there must be something specific that the schools in these jurisdictions do to deal with these diversities that affect teaching and learning (an issue also explored in Chapters 3 and 5). For the sake of comparison let us take a quick look at how Finnish schools cope with different learners with often significantly varying readiness to learn successfully in school.

Early and Immediate Intervention
In Alberta and Finland, equity in education is an important feature in school education – equity is seen as the key driver of excellence. It means more than just opening access to an equal education for all. As this book describes, equity in education is a principle that aims at guaranteeing high-quality education for all in different places and circumstances. In the Finnish context, equity is about having a socially fair and inclusive education system that is based on equality of outcomes and narrowing the opportunity gap in schools. Convincing evidence of more equitable learning outcomes came from the OECD's first PISA results in 2000. In that study, Finland had the smallest performance variations between schools in reading, mathematics, and science of all OECD nations. A similar trend

continued in the 2003 PISA cycle and was even strengthened in the PISA surveys of 2006 and 2009.

Although equity is an important principle in both Alberta and Finland, it is addressed in different ways within these systems. An essential element of the Finnish way of enhancing equity in schools is systematic attention to those students who have special educational needs. Special education is an important part of education and care in Finland, often called its 'educational flagship'. It refers to designed educational and psychological services within the education sector for those with special needs. The basic idea is that with early recognition of learning difficulties and social and behavioral problems, appropriate professional support can be provided to individuals as early as possible.

The aim of special education is to help and support students by giving them equal opportunities to complete school in accordance with their abilities and alongside their peers. There are two main pathways in special education in the Finnish comprehensive school. The first path sees the student included in a regular class and provided with *part-time special education* in small groups. A special education teacher leads these small groups, if the difficulties in learning are not serious. The student may also have an individual learning plan that adjusts the learning goals according to his or her abilities. Students with special educational needs may complete their studies following a regular or an adjusted curriculum. Student assessment is then based on the individual learning plan.

The second pathway is to provide *permanent special education* in a special group or class in the student's own school or, in some cases, in a separate institution. Transfer to special education in this case requires an official decision that is based on a statement by a psychological, medical, or social welfare professional, with a mandatory parental hearing. In Finland, the transfer decision to special needs education is made by the school board of the pupil's municipality of residence and can be processed rather quickly (within a few weeks in most cases). In order to promote success in learning, each student in special education has a personalized learning plan that is based on the school curriculum and adjusts educational expectations individually. This looks very different in Alberta (see Chapter 3).

In the school year 2011–2012, almost one third of all students in *Basic School* were enrolled in one of the two alternative forms of special education described above, a much higher proportion than in Alberta schools. About 23 percent of all Basic School students were in part-time special education that focuses on addressing minor dysfunctions in speaking, reading, and writing or learning difficulties in mathematics or foreign languages. The remaining nine percent of students were permanently transferred to a special education group, class, or institution. The number of students in permanent special education has doubled in the last 10 years; at the same time, the number of special education institutions has declined steadily since the early 1990s. This book states that support to children with special needs in Alberta has in recent years dramatically declined, according to the teachers. Finnish experience suggests that this is a worrying trend. Inclusion and high-quality special needs education seem to be integral parts of an equitable and high-performing school system.

In the early years of Basic School reform, Finland adopted a strategy of early intervention and prevention in helping those individuals who have special educational needs of some kind. This means that possible learning and development deficits are diagnosed and addressed during early childhood development and care before children enter school. In elementary grades, intensive special support, mostly in reading, writing, and arithmetic, is offered to all children who have major or minor learning difficulties. Therefore, the proportion of students in special education in Finland in the first three or four grades of primary school is relatively higher than in other countries and in Alberta. The number of special needs students in Finland declines by the end of primary school and then slightly increases as students move to subject-based lower secondary school. The reason for the increased need for special support in lower-secondary school in Finland is that the unified curriculum sets certain expectations for all students, regardless of their abilities or prior learning.

The highly equitable school system in Finland is not a result of educational factors alone. Basic structures of the Finnish welfare state play a crucial role in providing all children and their families with equitable conditions for starting a successful educational path at the age of seven. Early childhood care, voluntary free preschool that is attended by almost all of the six-year-olds' age cohort, comprehensive health services, and preventive measures to identify possible learning and development difficulties before children start schooling are accessible to all in Finland. Alberta has many of these public services as well but not all of them. Finnish schools also provide all pupils with free and healthy lunches every day, regardless of their home socioeconomic situation. Child poverty is at a very low level, less than four percent of the child population compared with one in 10 poor children in Alberta. This suggests that smart education policies in Alberta should focus on universal early childhood development, well-being in school, and a whole-child approach in curriculum and assessment, which all are aspects of better equity in education.

Conclusion

This book looks at the comparison between Alberta and Finland (see especially Chapters 4 and 5), but does so as a way of highlighting just where Alberta is on its equity for excellence journey. The book also looks at the history of this journey (Chapter 2) and the challenges for this journey (J-C Couture's Foreword and the Epilogue). It is a journey that requires both constant focus and attention, a relentless commitment to equity as the driver of public policy and a concern to ensure that schools are truly a great place for all.

References

Sahlberg, P. 2011. *Finnish Lessons. What can the world learn from educational change in Finland?* New York, NY: Teachers College Press.

Sahlberg, P. 2012. A Model Lesson. Finland shows us how equal opportunity looks like. *American Educator*, 36(2), 20-27.

Foreword

Equity – The Path for Creating a Great School for *All*
J-C Couture, PhD
Associate Coordinator, Research The Alberta Teachers' Association

> *"Alberta is at a crossroads. We need a new vision of society, one that promotes quality of life, well-being, and community over individualism. Alberta needs to rebuild the foundation of collective commitment and caring for each other that this province was built on and was known for across the country."*
>
> — (Gibson, 2012, p. 40)

Alberta's Educational Palimpsest

As students of history well know, in ancient times (way before Twitter or even paper) when print materials were in short supply, it was a common practice to reuse animal hides and later parchment, to write-over previous texts with new material. These 'written-over' texts became known as a *"palimpsest"*.

As with many OECD jurisdictions, the Alberta government's policy related to equity and inclusion in Alberta schools represent much of the same principles of the palimpsest. As an example of human ingenuity, the palimpsest shares the quintessential human agency of continually re-occupying the same public space. In the case of Alberta, one of the wealthiest places on earth, the constant re-writing of our policies focused on equity and social justice brings into question our commitment to address social and economic disparity and its attendant problems: higher rates of violence, addictions, poorer health and the breakdown of community and social cohesion[1].

In terms of the K-12 education sector in this province, the inertia and inability to commit to comprehensive supports for inclusion – *a great school for all students* – has been evident through decades of seemingly endless policy reviews, studies and relative inaction. This is one of the key reasons for bringing together the authors in the chapters that follow. It is time to take action and rethink equity.

---

[1] This is a view advanced in a definitive exploration of these issues in Gibson, D. (2012) *Social Policy Framework for Alberta: Fairness and Justice for All*. Edmonton: Parkland Institute.

Since the current Alberta government came to power 40 years ago, some argue that significant gains have been made in Alberta in terms of re-defining the heart of what means to be an Albertan. To supporters of the current government's 21st century education reform agenda, driven by the vision "to inspire and enable students to achieve success and fulfillment as engaged thinkers and ethical citizens with an entrepreneurial spirit within an inclusive education system" (Alberta Education, p. 7, 2011), the preferred future is robust and unambiguous. While at times "fairness" and "access for all" have been advanced as key principles and values guiding *Inspiring Action in Education* (2011), to critics it is apparent that through its funding of private and charter schools and the privileging of public-private partnerships, the government continues to promote "choice" and "competition" over the values of community, responsibility and equity. In this view, such an education reform agenda represents an important paradox amidst growing disparity (in 2010 Alberta had the greatest economic disparity and poverty gap in Canada), environmental degradation and unsustainable growth (Gibson, 2012, p, 24.).[2]

The contributors to *Rethinking Equity* raise concerns and offer renewed hope regarding the vision of creating a great school for all, a major focus of a recent Alberta Teachers' Association (2012) research initiative.

The book's contributors tackle equity from multiple perspectives. The chapters that follow range from system-level analyses of government policies over previous decades to case studies of the impacts of specific policies and strategies such as inclusion, coded funding, and "accommodations" made in Alberta's testing programs   Still other chapters provide international perspectives including efforts to achieve equity in Finland and what, if anything, can be learned from partnerships to build system and school–level capacity. For example the Finnish education system, in contrast to Alberta's current emphasis on choice and competition, "has been built upon values grounded in equity, equitable distribution of resources rather than competition and choice" (Sahlberg 2011, 96).

---

[2] Poverty gap is a measure of the distance between average income and the level of income at the poverty line. In 2010, Alberta's poverty rate was 9.1 percent, the lowest in Canada, but the poverty gap was 22.7 percent.

"Inclusion Confusion" in Alberta Classrooms

Chris Gilham and John Williamson, writing in "Inclusion's Confusion in Alberta", offer a comprehensive review of inclusion policies in recent years and the various impacts of the pervasive medicalized model of disability and its accompanying policies and programs. One stark example, "the bounty phenomenon," saw the rapid rise in numbers of students identified as having disabilities given this was the only mechanism through which school authorities could acquire the additional funds to support students. For school leaders, faced with what society considers to be an 'exceptional' student, the choice is clear: either work within the limits of their current budgets, or initiate a referral process that leads to ever-increasing demands on school psychologists to work on assessments. Yet despite promising signals in the past two years with to address these and other systemic issues (i.e. as articulated in *Action on Inclusion*), progress appears to have stalled once again.

The challenges identified by Gilham and Williamson reflect those identified in ongoing Alberta Teachers' Association research. Longitudinal data collected over the past decade illustrates the government's long-standing difficulties to respond to the needs of the least advantaged in this province[3]. In terms of support for students with special needs, survey data since 2005 show that in the view of Alberta teachers support for students with special needs has declined dramatically. In 2005, 25 percent of teachers indicated support had "somewhat or significantly" declined with this climbing to 57 percent in 2013. In 2005 19 percent reported supports had "somewhat or significantly improved", but this proportion dropped to 10 percent by 2013. Initial improvements in support for students with special needs (immediately after the 2003 Commission on Learning) appear to have slipped after 2005.

---

[3] An analysis of the Association's annual Member Survey is available in *The Courage to Choose Emerging Trends and Strategic Possibilities for Informed Transformation in Alberta Schools: 2010-2011.* Edmonton: Barnett House.

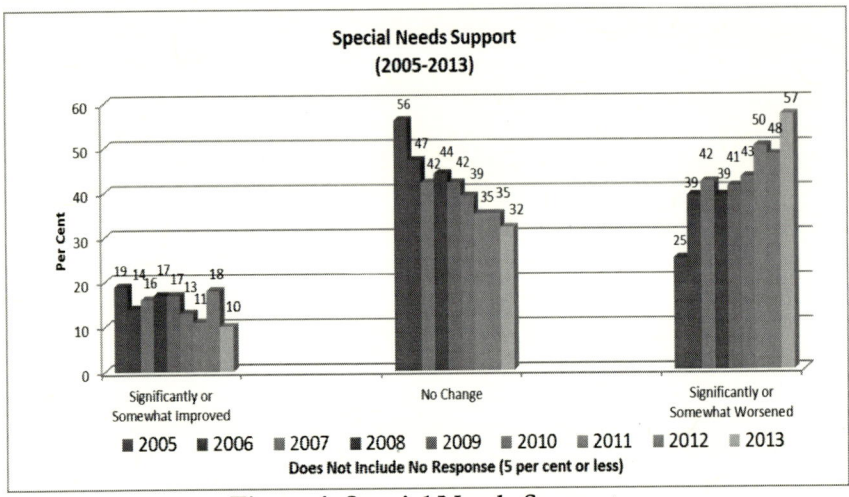

Figure 1: Special Needs Support

The commitment to equity through a focus on inclusion in schools is predicated on the assumption that a growing province such as Alberta provides the resources necessary to address both the growing and increasingly diverse and complex student population. Yet as we look at class size from 2005 to 2013, deterioration is evident. In 2013, 47 percent of Alberta teachers reported worsening class sizes compared to 16 percent in 2005. What is evident from the data is that despite some initial progress from 2005-2007 in addressing class size issues, there has been a marked decline since 2008.

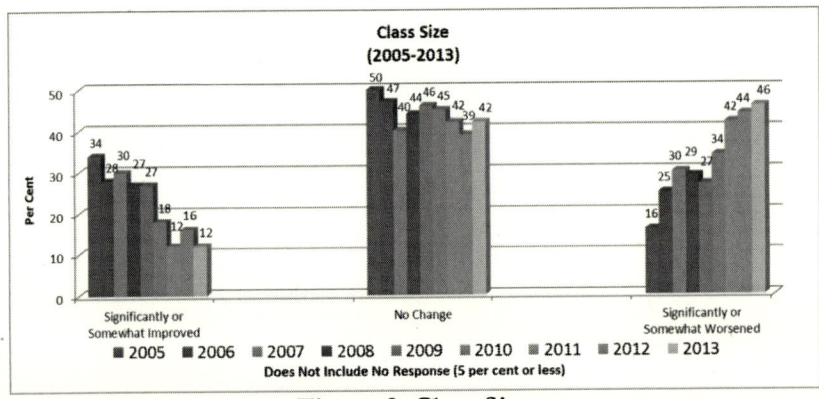

Figure 2: Class Size

Given Alberta's dramatic population growth (there will be five million Albertans in 2020) is one indicator of the vibrancy of the province and its long-term prospects for economic growth. Along with this growth comes a diversity that is both an asset and a challenge for schools. As we look back over the period 2008-13, when asked about the growing range and complexity of student learning needs, in 2005 20 percent of Alberta teachers reported "somewhat or significant" worsening conditions rising to 58 percent by 2013 –an almost three-fold decline.

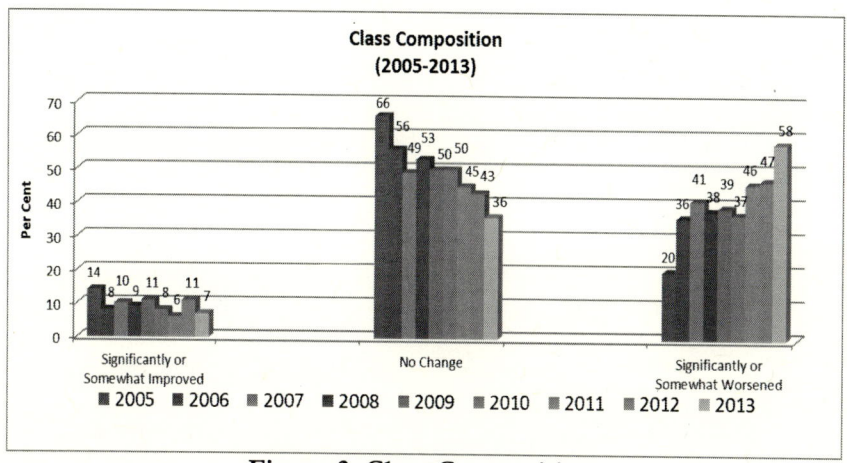

Figure 3: Class Composition

These data, in the context of other broader demographic realities, illustrate that we are we not investing in capitalizing on the growing asset of our increasingly diverse population. Between 1991 and 2011, Alberta's population grew by over 1.1 million – going from 9.9% of Canada's population to 10.9%. As we go to press, Alberta's population is set to tip the four million mark and projected to reach five million by 2020. In 2012, of the 200,000 new Albertans, 35,764 were immigrants from 200 different countries[4]. With the majority of new Albertans between the ages of 18 and44, it is no surprise that the 52,398 babies born last year in Alberta exceeded those of British Columbia's by 10,000.

Alberta's demographic watershed clearly offers much promise for the future of the growth and vibrancy of the education sector. Yet currently the

---

[4] Paula Simons, Population growth will change Alberta forever, *Edmonton Journal*, Saturday, July 6, 2012, A13.

number one sources of stress for Alberta teachers is the "unmet needs of my students"[5], particularly those representing vulnerable populations.

Equity: Alberta's Unfulfilled Promise

As a number of the contributors outline in the chapters that follow, a good start in achieving inclusion in Alberta schools would be to begin peeling away the long history and many layers of government studies and pronouncements about equity, rather than focusing on empirical evidence and funding structures that would actually get the supports to the students that need them most.

Critically evaluating a society's commitment to supporting living and learning in the early years of life is the foundational pillars of equity. This is one of the key implications of "Two models of 'Education for all' - A comparative view on the inclusive and special education policies in Alberta and Finland" by Markku Jahnukainen. As he illustrates, the Finnish model of 'education for all' targets the lowest-achieving students and tries to improve the overall standard from there. In other words, the main strategy is to maintain equity and quality education in every school through the comprehensive public school system and supports for early learning. But rather than simplistically edifying the Finnish schools, he describes how both high-performing jurisdictions have much to learn from each other, particularly around supporting local decision-making and teacher autonomy.

In the view of Alberta teachers, student readiness to learn continues to be a persistent area of concern. Despite years of policy reviews, promises of 'wrap-around services', learning coaches, digitized student profiling platforms and other commitments outlined in the *Action on Inclusion*, the realities of roller-coaster funding, including a freeze on increases in special education funding, have taken their toll. For example, as the data indicate, in 2006, 36 percent of teachers reported a decline in student readiness to learn with this number rising to 45 percent in 2011 and 57 percent in 2013.

---

[5] 2013 Member Survey. Alberta Teachers' Association. Edmonton: Barnett House. Approximately 80% rate this source as a "high" (38.4 percent) or "moderate" (40.8 percent) source of stress.

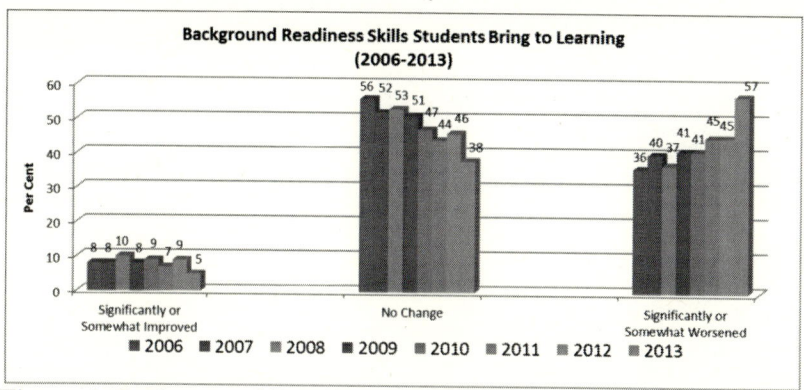

Figure 4: Background Readiness Skills Students Bring to Learning

For Albertans, the fallout from years of government's continual re-writing of policies and subsequent inaction occurred November 2012, with the release of the independent national "Early Years Study", authored by Margaret McCain, Dr. Fraser Mustard, who died a week before the report was released, and Kerry McCuaig. Their research study provides the social, economic and scientific rationale for public investment in young children and recommends that all children be entitled to an early education from age two. For children, the study says early education results in improved school readiness, graduation levels, future earnings and health.

The independent report ranked each province on the early education services they provide according to 15 benchmarks, which reflect a common set of core standards essential for the delivery of quality programming. Benchmarks were organized into five categories: governance, funding, access, learning environment, and accountability. Each category is given three points for a total of 15. Standings by province in the Early Childhood Education Index (ECI) out of 15 points are indicated in the table below. Resource-rich Alberta is second last out of 10 provinces.

Province	Score	% of ECI
Quebec	10	67
Prince Edward Island	9.5	63
Manitoba	7.5	50
Ontario	6.5	43
Nova Scotia	5.0	33
British Columbia	4.5	30

Saskatchewan	4.5	30
New Brunswick	4.5	30
Alberta	3.0	20
Newfoundland	1.5	10

Table 1: Standings by Province in the Early Childhood Education Index out of 15

As a province, Alberta cannot afford to ignore the ongoing structural obstacles related to the readiness to learn. Guaranteed universal access to early childhood education and a comprehensive community-based approach to enhancing the well-being of children and youth are essential to achieving the vision of the government's *Inspiring Action* agenda. Current piece-meal government policies aimed at addressing readiness to learn continue to fall short. As reported in a recent report by Public Interest Alberta, Head Start executive director Kathy Lenihan points out that the provincial preschool program for low-income families turns away 900 needy families each year. She said children from impoverished families suffer high levels of dental problems, learning delays and interpersonal troubles, partly because parents are stressed and working and do not have adequate supports.

At home, complacency is also our worst enemy. As Stephen Murgatroyd's contribution in Chapter 1 notes, one out of every 10 Alberta children lives in poverty, 42,800 of them school-age children[6], yet Albertans are materially among the richest people on the planet as measured by GDP per capita. The downstream impacts of public policies that ignore the systemic day-to-day problems faced by Alberta's children and youth require courageous and decisive action. The persistent inequities faced by marginalized groups such as First Nations are slowly being addressed through such measures as a Memorandum of Understanding for First Nations Education in Alberta with Treaty 6, 7 and 8 that represent comprehensive government-to-government agreements on implementing poverty reduction strategies (Hudson, 2012, pp. 34-35).

There are other signs of progress. Recent moves by the Alberta government such as publication of the Early Development Instrument (EDI) community mapping project of readiness to learn indicators available for 2009-2012 surveyed groups—all indicators of a shifting agenda. The fact that

---

[6] There are 91,000 children living in poverty in the province with 53 percent under the age of six living in this category (Hudson, 2012, p. 9).

most Alberta communities have received their first findings, based on this tool developed in British Columbia[7] in collaboration with kindergarten teachers, marks an unprecedented opportunity for equity to move beyond an abstract policy concept to a concrete action.

Yet, equity and government inclusion strategies continue to be a text written and re-written every day in Alberta classrooms. For example, Alberta teachers continue to contribute $1,000 per year out of their own pockets to purchasing school materials and classroom resources. Indeed, 60 percent of teachers reported in 2012 that they could not carry out their teaching assignment without purchasing materials out of their own pockets. As well, gender plays a role, although largely silent, in the day-to-day 'inclusion' story in Alberta classrooms. As the Association's annual Member Survey and the recent study of teachers in the first five years of practice documents[8], younger, female teachers are the most likely to be providing their students with subsidized materials and supports out of their own pockets. Indeed, teachers with early childhood services and elementary assignments and classroom only responsibilities are the most likely to feel a need to subsidize their school's budget with their own financial resources.

School Leadership for Excellence Through Equity

It is no accident that many of the contributors in this book are classroom teachers or research-practitioners working directly alongside classroom teachers. These contributors straddle between the day-to-day lived experiences of the local school-community while drawing upon a variety of boundary and system-crossing experiences. In "Perspectives of Inclusion:

---

[7] The Early Development Instrument (EDI) is an early child development questionnaire developed by Dr. Dan Offord and Dr. Magdalena Janus at the Offord Centre for Child Studies at McMaster University. http://earlylearning.ubc.ca/edi/. To date, more than 700 early child development initiatives and community projects have been supported by EDI results. Examples include Preschooler Health Day Circuits in Prince George and the hiring of early childhood educators for preschools and daycares in Vancouver Island neighbourhoods. In Alberta, under the direction of Alberta Education's Early Learning branch, the ECD Mapping Initiative is guided by a contracted project team, based at the University of Alberta. The Early Child Development Mapping Project (ECMap) is working with communities to gather information about local programs and services that support healthy child development.

[8] Alberta Teachers' Association (2012). *Teaching in the Early Years of Practice: A Five-Year Longitudinal Study.* Edmonton, AB: Barnett House.

Sketches of Beginning Possibilities in an Alberta-Finland Partnership," as a school jurisdiction leader, Kathy Olmstead sees real possibilities in lessons learned from Finland, where the emphasis is on building the capacity for local decision-making and the role of principals is supporting teacher autonomy and professional responsibility. Rather than focusing on accountabilities, coding structures and reporting back to a centralized authority, local communities are enabled to offer the supports deemed necessary based on a commitment to equity for all.

In their chapter, "The Level Playing Field: Unconcealing Diploma Exam Accommodation Policy" by examining the impacts of standardized high-stakes testing and testing accommodations for learners with diagnosed disabilities in Alberta, John Williamson and Jim Paul critically assess the myth of the accommodations metaphor of "leveling the playing field." As their analysis uncovers, the taken-for-granted assumptions of testing practices that allow for more flexible assessment conditions for all students would, for many students with disabilities, strip away "governance of disability." As well, breaking-open the language of accommodations would help to question the normalization of the government's testing programs.

Leadership in Equity and Excellence: Not a 'Zero-Sum Game'

> "The staggering truth is, almost everything that we've accomplished in the 20th century can be attributed to our public education system."
>
> - Lois Hole, former Lieutenant-Governor of Alberta

A recent research review of school leadership in Alberta, co-published by the Association, argues that the attributes of teacher leadership that would support the creation of a great school for all Alberta students would be the very same qualities we would directly or indirectly expect of all of leaders across all public policy sectors (Murgatroyd and Couture, 2012). In sort, the public policy challenges facing education reform in the coming years will impact all sectors of Alberta society:

1. How do we ensure equity for all learners – no matter what their home conditions, physical or mental challenges or levels of support in the community?

2. How do we provide learning pathways which meet the different needs of different learners while at the same time ensuring the quality of all learning taking place in the school?

3. How do we leverage the assets of a community to enable all to learn in a school?

4. How do we utilize technology to support engaged and inclusive learning for all?

5. How do we enable schools to design learning pathways for each student so that their ambitions, hopes and opportunities are realized? (2012, p. 7).

For Albertans, the society-building project of simultaneously supporting excellence and equity in education is a fundamental leadership challenge shared by all Canadians.

Allen Gregg, one of this country's most respected political observers, has noted that increasingly Canadians have been convinced of a new narrative where "we seem to be living in a zero-sum society" characterized by "a politics of polarization, over-torqued partisanship and dogma." This new 'zero sum' story where opportunity is framed as shrinking for everyone not only partly explains the anger of the Occupy Movement or the students protesting in the streets of Montreal but also the growing "disdain that the middle class has for "pampered" public sector employees or the excessive obsession the rich seem to have about the poor "ripping off the system." The downstream effect, Gregg argues, is a citizenry increasingly convinced that governments are powerless and that equity and social justice will remain ephemeral goals. Now that we are caught in the post-2008 economic maelstrom we are at risk of turning against ourselves, becoming as Gregg describes, "a fearful divided citizenry."

Last year in Canada, the top 10% of the working population earned on average $165,322 in contrast to an average of $9,750 after tax for the bottom 10%. While in the past 30 years the average income for the top 10% increased in 34%, the increase for the bottom 10% was only 11%. This perceived 'shrinking pie' is leading to a new age of imposed austerity and a major rethink of spending across Canada. While doing comparatively better than most countries following the 2008 meltdown, our country is not immune. Public services across the board including education are under attack and will be challenged to sustain their resource base. The resulting pressure is already evident across all education sectors in Alberta.

The choice ahead for Alberta is not a zero-sum game. Consider that Albertans are materially ranked as in the top five richest people on the planet. From 2005 to 2008, Alberta churned out $229 billion worth of fossil fuels, the equivalent $30 million for every man, woman and child (Hudson, 2013, p. 35). Against this reality, Alberta continues to have the lowest rate of taxation across the country. If Alberta increased its taxation revenues by $11 billion per year, the province would still retain its position as the lowest tax jurisdiction in the country (p. 35). While poverty is costing the province $7.1 to 9.5 billion per year, it is estimated that 50% of this amount would eradicate the issue (p. 35) with the cost dropping over time.

The downstream impacts of public policies that marginalize and ignore the systemic day-to-day problems faced by Alberta's children and youth require courageous and decisive leadership both in our schools and community at large if we are to achieve the goal of creating a great school for all. The chapters in this collection underscore the cross-road we are at in terms of supporting inclusion and a great school for all students as a pillar for achieving equity in Alberta schools.

References

Alberta Education. (2011). *Inspiring Action on Education*. Edmonton. http://ideas.education.alberta.ca/media/2905/inspiringaction%20eng.pdf

Alberta Teachers' Association. (2012). *A Great School for All – Transforming Education in Alberta*. Edmonton, AB: Barnett House.

Duxbury, L. (2012). *Work life of Alberta teachers - A national study*. Presentation, Calgary, AB. November 1, 2012.

Gibson, D. (2012) *Social Policy Framework for Alberta: Fairness and Justice for All*. Edmonton, AB: Parkland Institute.

Gregg, A. (2012). http://www.huffingtonpost.ca/2012/09/10/allan-gregg-speech-assault-on-reason_n_1871658.html

Hargreaves, A., Fink, D. (2006). *Sustainable Leadership*. San Francisco, CA: Jossey-Bass.

Hudson, Carol-Anne. (2012). *Poverty Costs 2.0: Investing in Albertans*. Calgary, AB: Vibrant Communities Calgary and Action to End Poverty in Alberta.

Kanter, R.M. (1977). *Men and women of the corporation*. New York, NY: Basic Books.

Murgatroyd, S. and Couture, J-C. 2012. *Rethinking School Leadership: Creating Great Schools for All Students*. Edmonton, AB: *future*THINK Press.

Sahlberg, P. 2011. *Finnish Lessons: What Can the World Learn from Educational Change in Finland?* New York, NY: Teachers College Press.

Chapter 1: The Future and Equity
Stephen Murgatroyd, PhD FRSA FBPsS

CEO, Collaborative Media Group and Chief Scout, the Innovation Expedition Inc.

Introduction

Fifty Seven million children world-wide are "out of school" despite the fact that they deserve to be in primary education. While real progress is being made towards the Millennium Development Goal of achieving universal compulsory primary education, Malala Yousafzai's call at the United Nations in July 2013 for every child to have "a book, a pen and a teacher" has yet to be answered. When Alberta looks outward at what is happening in the world and how we can learn from these developments, we should begin with understanding that many countries are seeking to secure basic access to elementary school learning – meantime, we are seeking to sustain our global leadership in education.

These are challenging times[1]. Whether it is the shifting fortunes of the oil and gas sector and its impact on Alberta's finances, uncertainty about power and democracy in Alberta, concerns about the plight of the disadvantaged in Alberta or issues about Alberta's environmental sustainability, it is clear that Alberta is changing along with the world around it. So as to understand equity in a broad context, there is a need to understand the pattern of change that is taking place around the world – the dynamics of the future – so that we can understand how equity becomes a critical driver for that future. The future of Alberta is a contested space. Understanding what is driving the future will help us better champion equity in this contest. By looking globally at development, we can better understand our local challenges.

There are five key developments that we can see when we look around the world. Here each is briefly described, with information and data about the development and a look at the implications each development may have for

---

[1] Part of this chapter appeared in the Fall 2013 edition of The *Alberta Teachers' Association Magazine*.

our thinking about the future of schooling in Alberta. These developments will also impact equity.

Austerity

Wherever we look in Canada and in the developed world, governments face financial challenges which are leading to significant issues for schools, colleges and universities. Britain, for example, is looking at several decades of austerity and the situation in most of Europe is serious, especially in Portugal, Ireland, Greece and Spain (the so-called PIGS economies) – only Germany and Austria are posting significant economic growth; all other EU nations are fiscally challenged. Many US States and South American countries (Brazil, Argentina, for example) are also finding it necessary to scale back the rate of investment and growth of public education, hence the attraction of social enterprise and private sector engagement in school systems.

In France, 60,000 secondary school teaching positions were cut during the period 2006-12, and the present French Presidency intends to continue to reduce public expenditure in all areas, including education, by $19CAN billion (14 billion Euros).

One consequence of the widespread adoption of austerity is youth unemployment. In France, 1.9 million young people (15-29 year olds) are not in education or employment. More than half of those aged 18-25 in Greece and Spain are out of work, and the overall level of youth unemployment for the EU has now reached 5.6 million - 24% of those aged 15-24. In the US, youth unemployment is 17% of this same age group. Alberta, which has compulsory education to age 16 but now permits attendance to age 18, has an unemployment rate of 8.5%.

As austerity deepens in many countries, youth becomes disillusioned with schooling and the link between their education and the ability to obtain work. Governments are looking at addressing these challenges by a combination of training and work-placement schemes, but the underlying challenge is the strength of economic activity in a jurisdiction. Equity is threatened by the inequity of economic life.

Privatization, Social Enterprise and Public Good

England is rapidly moving to a corrupted social enterprise model for the delivery of learning at all levels of its education system. By January 2013, some 2,600 English schools (12% of all schools and over 50% of all English high schools) had opted out of the control of Local Education Authorities (equivalent to an Alberta School Board) and are free to set their own admission standards, recruit teachers to teach (including teachers without a teaching qualification), set teacher pay levels and receive the same funds as a publicly managed school would receive. There are 28 local authorities where at least one in five schools is now an open academy. In almost all of the 129 local authorities, at least one in five secondary schools is an open academy. There are 10 local authorities where at least one in five primary schools is now an open primary academy. Schools are converting all the time – by May of 2013 an additional 150 schools had converted.

At this time academies are not-for-profit organizations. The ruling Conservative Party has made clear that, should they win an outright majority in the next election in May 2015, academies can elect to become for profit organizations. Similar developments are occurring in Sweden, where Free Schools have been operating since 1992. By 2010 some 75% of Swedish school students attended a school owned and operated by a for-profit company, subsidized by the States grant of per pupil funding.

Not all is well in Sweden. In 2013 JB Education, which supports the education of over 10,000 students in Free Schools in Sweden, indicated that it was to close several of its schools since it could no longer fund these "loss making operations". Some of Sweden's private school companies operate schools in the UK.

Charter schools are similar to academies in England and Free Schools in Sweden. Alberta has just 13 Charter Schools, all of which are not for profit.

Private-sector investments in education K-12 are rising. Both Pearson and News Corp are now investing directly in owning school systems, and other investments are focused on technology. In the US alone in 2012 educational investment topped $1 billion, including investments in post-secondary education systems.

So as to continue to secure funding, many academies, free schools and charter schools "game" the system. They carefully select students who will provide results which attract the most funding and do not admit students who will increase costs or cause the overall performance of the school to fall even by a fraction of a percentage. They also game the system in other ways. Privatization and marketization pose risks to an education system founded on equity.

Learning Analytics, Value Added and Personalization

The use of data to track learning and performance and for the assessment of the teachers' contribution to that learning is big business around the world. The City of New York released data on about 18,000 individual math and English teachers' performance. The Teacher Data Reports ranked teachers based on their students' gains on the state's math and English tests over the course of five years (up until the 2009–2010 academic year). Proponents of value-added assessment — that includes US Secretary of Education Arne Duncan and former NYC School Chancellor (and now head of News Corp's education division) Joel Klein — argue that this model demonstrates teachers' effectiveness, and as such should be used to help determine how to compensate teachers, as well as who to fire. The US spends some $1.7 billion each year testing K-12 students and an increasing level of expenditure on formalized and public assessments of teachers.

Using student assessment data also enables, according to some, the personalization of learning. Analytics are at the heart of the work of the Khan Academy and of many of the developments in what is known as "adaptive" learning, where what a student studies and what materials they are provided for this work is shaped by their assessment data. Software programs using machine intelligence, such as *Knewton*, have been developed to support this work. The vision is simple: within five or 10 years, the paper textbook and mimeographed worksheet will be dead. Classroom exercises and homework—text, audio, video, games—will have shifted entirely to the iPad or equivalent. Adaptive learning will help each user find the exact right piece of content needed, in the exact right format, at the exact right time, based on previous patterns of use and currently assessed abilities for each individual student. Students can move at their own speed. They can get hints and instant feedback. Teachers, meanwhile, can spend class time targeting their help to individuals or small groups based on need.

School boards find these developments seductive. They can mine the big data sets concerning performance and look at their "return on investment" from new curriculum developments, teachers and technology. The fact that there are doubts about the use of these data is secondary to the fact of being able to see "evidence".

Access to and use of technology is an equity issue. Not all learners can afford or are easily able to use technology. While some technologies, especially for students with disabilities, have been highly enabling, others can be labeled "disabling".

The Digital Revolution

The combination of new learning devices – tablet technologies, Smart Phones and Smart Boards – and the emergence of open education resources (OER'S) – free to use learning materials, simulations, games, textbooks, worksheets, animations – are enabling learning with the support of technology to be commonplace. The Indian Government is promoting the use of tablets as an effective medium for learning, with over 50 models receiving their financial support. By 2014 all textbooks required to complete a K-12 education in the State of Kerala will be available on tablets for free – other Indian states are also pursuing similar objectives.

It is not just textbooks that are going digital. Learners can access simulations, educational games and assessment activities online via hand-held devices. Students can also engage in video or audio conferences, develop and share presentations, track and complete projects and complete assignments.

If learners have access to powerful learning technologies that can adapt to the learners' levels of knowledge and understanding, what is it that teachers now do? The answer some would give is that they focus on coaching, guiding, mentoring and remediation rather than instruction. The technology supports provide instruction – knowledge, skill development – the teacher provides support and creates opportunities for learners to demonstrate their learning in practice. This is the essence of the "flipped classroom" – an outcropping of the digital revolution. The suggestion is that the technology does not replace teaching; it enables teachers to play a different role in their relationship to both students and knowledge.

To date, there's no scientific research base to indicate exactly how well flipped classrooms work. But some preliminary non-scientific data suggest that flipping the classroom may produce benefits. In one survey of 453 teachers who flipped their classrooms, 67 percent reported increased test scores, with particular benefits for students in advanced placement classes and students with special needs; 80 percent reported improved student attitudes; and 99 percent said they would flip their classrooms again next year (Flipped Learning Network, 2012). Clintondale High School in Michigan saw the failure rate of its 9th grade math students drop from 44 to 13 percent after adopting flipped classrooms (Finkel, 2012).

In many parts of the world, building schools and offering classes with one teacher for each group of 30-40 students is simply not possible due to the scale of public investment needed. Open Schools which use open and distance learning, ICT and open education resources are a fast-growing response to this challenge, with the Commonwealth of Learning (based in Vancouver) leading this work. Using materials developed nationally and adapted locally, radio and ICT access to primary and secondary education is made possible with considerable success.

These developments represent the other side of the technology coin. While access to and support for technology can be an equity issue, its use can also enable equitable access for many to an education and educational resources which would otherwise have been impossible, and technology can also provide the opportunity for equity.

STEM and the Curriculum

The curriculum focus on science, technology, engineering and mathematics (STEM subjects) is regarded by many as of growing importance, with some parents demanding that their sons and daughters take more STEM and less of other subjects. Their understanding is that the future of work relies heavily on STEM and that other subjects will "distract" students from those studies most likely to produce economic returns. On a recent visit to Singapore, the number one challenge faced by Secondary School Principals is the demands of parents for STEM to be the *only* subjects on the curriculum.

One consequence of this is that creative and fine arts, physical education, music, dance, literature and writing are seen as less important and often disappear from the curriculum as a student moves from elementary school through the system. Yet one of the fastest-growing sectors of the global economy involves design and the creative economy (gaming, movie making, television, web-design, simulations, architecture, interior design etc.). In the UK, the creative economy is generating a faster rate of job growth than manufacturing, and across the EU the creative industries now account for 4% of the EU's GDP.

Steve Jobs was fond of saying that Apple's success was due to the fact that rather than employing geeks, they hired, in his words, "poets, musicians and artists who are interested in technology". The 21st Century curriculum movement is in danger of too strongly focusing on STEM at the expense of other learning and, as a framework for entrepreneurship, misses out on fast growth sectors.

The Overall Position – GERM versus Equity

Schooling is changing world-wide, in part due to economics and in part due to technology. But at the heart of education the challenge remains the same. How do we build meaningful and mindful relationships between students, teachers and knowledge? How do we make sense of the global changes described above, and others that impact our schools, communities and socio-economic well-being?

We can see a tension between two competing visions for the school systems of the future. We refer to one as the global education reform movement (GERM)[2] and the other as an equity-driven vision.

GERM

The global education reform movement is driven by a view of education as serving the economic needs of a jurisdiction. The language of this framework is one of competencies, skills and knowledge needed for the workforce and to sustain and grow a vibrant and diverse economy. It is mingled with the language of business – accountability, productivity, performance and management – which is not surprising, since many of those advancing this view are corporations (CISCO, Microsoft, News Corporation, Pearson and others, who also have a stake in providing solutions to this movement). While GERM is especially strong in K-12 education, it is also now permeating training and post-secondary education world-wide.

At its heart, GERM involves these ideas:

- Learning can be broken down into competencies and competencies can be tested for using powerful and effective analytic tools.

- Learning not tied to competencies or skills needed for the economy is not worth substantial investment – creative arts, fine arts and sports are marginalized by a strong focus on science, technology, engineering and mathematics – the so called STEM subjects.

- Teachers are part of the problem not part of the solution – they need to be seen not as designers and creators of learning, but as facilitators of agreed curriculum. The idea that teachers are "professionals" gets in the way of efficiency, productivity and cost control. Teachers need to be better trained, managed and paid by the value they add to learning as measured by analytics.

---

[2] We are grateful to Pasi Sahlberg and Andy Hargreaves for coining this term.

- Curriculum needs to be standardized so that it is fair to all and we can test progress in standardized ways.

- Learning can and should be "personalized" – technology enables this (especially adaptive technologies), made easier when the curriculum is standardized – it makes testing and getting to scale easier.

- Teachers should make more use of technology so that they can better monitor student progress and mastery of competence and intervene when a student is seen (from analytic data) to be struggling.

- Education should be available anytime and anywhere – technology enables this.

- Institutions should be accountable for their learning outcomes and cost management – value added auditing should be undertaken.

- Market forces should determine "winners" and "losers", and parental choice should drive educational investment.

- Social enterprise in free markets is the best way to manage education.

Governments, like those in the UK, Australia and the US, are systematically pursuing GERM in their K-12 systems, and this is also having an impact on training, college and university education. Underlying this is the use of business models to manage and run institutions, as if private business knew how to deliver efficient and effective public education. Institutions which adopt GERM tend to have a high manager-to-teacher ratio, high technology costs and at the end of the day, very little evidence of real improvements in learning outcomes. GERM is also a vendor-driven strategy which governments are finding attractive. At the heart of these developments is a shift in the management of education from public ownership for public good to private ownership for profit and corporate gain.

Equity-Based Educational Systems

An alternative framework, also competing for a major slice of the future, sees the work schools very differently. Rather than focusing on the "products" of schooling in terms of the workplace competencies and skills, this approach sees education as an opportunity to enable and encourage the pursuit of bold, big ideas and to develop the person as a citizen, imaginer and life-long learner. It is also seen as a way of creating real opportunities to promote and support the public good and well-being of society and community through enhancing the ability of learners to think critically and develop a life-long passion for learning for learning's sake.

Rather than being competency-driven and focused on competitive skills, this approach sees learning as a fundamental process in support of a more equitable, informed and empowered community / society in which informed and engaged citizens lead a quality of life which has meaning for them.

The key ingredients of this approach are:

- A focus on the learner as a whole person, not just as a potential employee or "contributing citizen".

- A focus on understanding, engagement, knowledge and skills – balancing these different aspects of the task of learning and understanding.

- An understanding that the key to such learning is the teacher (or team of teachers), and these must be empowered to align available resources to the needs of the learner.

- Rather than having a strong focus on accountability, this approach favours assurance and assessment focused on helping the learner improve their learning.

- The teacher and the communities of practice to which she belongs are central to this approach to learning. Rather than "follow" the script of a master course, here teachers as professionals tailor their learning designs and activities to the needs of the individual students in their class. Working with a curriculum framework, the teacher as professional is enabled and empowered as a designer of learning.

- In the name of equity, there is a strong focus on inclusion and accessibility – rather than continuously increasing the GPA needed to "get in" to college or university, institutions and programs look more to commitment, determination and engagement.

- Attention is paid to the support needs of learners – additional help is available for those struggling with concepts or skills or who need additional help because of a learning, or other, disability.

- Compassion, mindfulness and empathy and support are seen to be core to learning outcomes.

- Technology can be used to support these overall activities, but is not seen as a driver or "the answer".

This set of ideas provides a very different philosophical base for the work of schools – leading to very different designs for learning, assessment and curriculum.

Many attempts are being made to focus on equity not just in terms of access but also in terms of success in education – it as at the heart of the UNESCO's work on rethinking education, for example as well as being at the core of UNESCO Delors' Commission four pillars of education (UNESCO. It competes with GERM for the ideological standing as the base for strategic policy and investment decisions by Government.

Equity as the Challenge for All of Our Futures

One key barrier to overcome in this "in between" time is the growing fact of inequity in developed societies, especially those with significant wealth, such as Alberta. A key issue for the future of Canada will be how to bridge the increasing gap between the rich and the poor, those with advanced literacy skills (level 3 and above) versus those with poor skills (Levels 1 and 2 or an inability to read and engage in basic cognitive processes), those born into poverty and those born into wealth, those with disabilities and those without, and between First Nations people and all others.

The facts are clear for Canada:

- Between 1980 and 2011, the top 10% of the working population by earnings earned on average $165,322 after tax (a 34% rise over this time.)

- Between 1980 and 2011, the bottom 10% of the working population by earnings earned on average $9,750 after tax (an 11% rise over this time.)

The Alberta statistics are also clear:

- In Alberta, 148,000 non-elderly families and 73,000 children experienced income inequality in 2011. 34,000 of those children were below the age of six.

- According to 2011 Statistics Canada data, 300,000 Albertans fall below the low income (after-tax) cut-off – the measure of poverty. 13% of all families in Calgary and 16% of all families in Edmonton.

- The Conference Board of Canada (2011) found that Alberta's low-income rate increased from 6.6 to 9.9 percent between 2009 and 2011.

- Over two-thirds of low-wage workers in Alberta are women. More women work in low-wage non-standard occupations than men, usually for low pay, without any benefits and without qualifying for employment insurance.

At the heart of inequality is education, in particular, literacy. When we look at the impact of education on the ability to work and earn, we see that there is a growing demand for workers that hold a post-secondary qualification. Linda Duxbury, in her studies of Canadian demography (Dyke and Duxbury, 2011), observes that some 70% of jobs now require post-secondary qualification – a college diploma or a university degree. This requirement is expected to rise to 77% by 2031 (Miner, 2012). Currently, 60% of Canada's workforce has a post-secondary qualification.

The difference in earnings between those who leave school without a high school diploma (average earnings $21,200) and those with a degree (average earnings $48,600) is and will continue to be substantial, as is the ability to increase earnings over time amongst those with post-secondary education – the higher the qualification, the higher the earning power (OECD, 2013). While some with degrees are finding it difficult to obtain employment, the overall unemployment rate for graduates across the OECD is five percent% - the same as it has been for over three decades.

This income disparity is especially a challenge for those from First Nations. The strongest performance by students with registered Indian status who wrote the Provincial Achievement Test was in Grade 3. Over the past two years to 2012, approximately 40% of Grade 3 students in band-operated schools and 50-70% of aboriginal students in other school systems met the Acceptable Standard in English language arts and mathematics. The weakest performance was in Grade 9. In the past three years, fewer than 15% of Grade 9 students in band-operated schools and fewer than 50% of students in other school systems met the Acceptable Standard in mathematics, science and social studies. While this measurement data exists, these observations cannot be generalized to all students with registered Indian status in the province due to the low student participation rate in the Achievement Testing Program, especially at the Grade 9 level.

Given that the aboriginal student population is fast growing, the rising inequity between First Nations people and other Canadians is a source of social tension. The unemployment rate for First Nations is twice that for other Albertans. Just over 33% of aboriginals in the workforce have no post-secondary qualification, and only 6.7% hold a first degree.

Given the pattern of educational outcomes in Canada, it is likely that Canada will experience major challenges in securing the skills needed to sustain its economy. Many analysts suggests that by 2021 Canada could be short approximately 2.6 million workers due to decreasing fertility rates, an ageing population, and the skill gap between the output of the education system and the demands of employees. Unless we improve our productivity, this figure could reach 4.2 million by 2031 (Milner, 2012).

The Canadian Council on Learning (2011) has also indicated that there is a clear "gap between the demand for workers with strong literacy and numeracy skills and the supply of Canadians who possess them." The Council points out that the growth in the information communication technology industries, coupled with the reduced demand for unskilled workers due to foreign outsourcing, has only intensified the need for skilled workers.

We must question why there is such a skills gap, since Canadian teenagers traditionally do well on Programme for International Assessment (PISA) tests, and on various other measures of educational outcomes. The answer, some speculate, lies in the failure of adults to keep up with the "demands of the emerging knowledge society and information economy." In other words, lifelong learning is as essential to a strong economy as successful schools. As is demonstrated in the OECD's *Education at a Glance* statistics on adult participation in education and learning, job-related training is comparatively low in Canada.

For literacy, the data is most disconcerting:

- 42% of the Canadian population — nine million people — between the ages of 16 and 65 have literacy levels that do not permit full engagement in a knowledge-based society.

- In Alberta, the absolute numbers of adults with skills below Level 3 is projected to grow from 1,051,413 (2006) to 1,233,000 (2016), or 17%.

- Overall, 46% of employed Alberta workers have a literacy skill deficit.

- 18 Alberta industries function with 50% or more of their employees having literacy levels below that demanded by their jobs.

- One third of young employed persons have literacy skills below the level required for their occupation.

- 59% of immigrants in the experienced labour force have a literacy skill deficit compared to 43% of their non-immigrant peers.

These statistics are even more disconcerting given the frequent testing of learning outcomes in Alberta. It is not that reading is absent, but rather comprehension, critical and adaptive thinking, and in-depth understanding are in short supply.

Literacy, as defined here, is a major source of inequality: low literacy skills limit employee promotion and advancement in employment and labour mobility are inhibited.

Canada and Alberta have a growing gap between rich and poor, and between those with high literacy skills and lower literacy skills. A skills shortage will occur even though there will be individuals searching for work. The gap between searchers and those who find employment will be focused on educational attainment and literacy.

Education and Equity

These data and our understanding of their dynamics suggest that equity is a major challenge for our society as development occurs. And, as the gap between rich and poor grows, fuelled by educational attainment and literacy, we will see growing challenges to the viability of organizations, communities and occupations – all placed under stress by the forces described at the beginning of this chapter (see also Murgatroyd, 2012). But, there is another form of equity we should be conscious of – the equity between schools in terms of their ability to make a difference to student learning.

One the claims of the Finnish system, documented in Pasi Sahlberg's book *Finnish Lessons* (Sahlberg, 2011) , is that the learning outcomes achieved by schools in Finland show little difference between them. In fact, Sahlberg goes further to suggest that variance within a school in terms of performance is greater than the variance between them. He suggests that this is a critical component of the Finnish school system – the lack of significant differences in outcomes between schools means that there is geographic equity (outcomes are not dependent on where you live or which school you attend) as well as actual equity. He views equity as a major thrust for educational policy.

This between-school equity is not the case in other jurisdictions. In the UK, for example, there is a vast difference in outcomes between one school and another, reflecting both the "inputs" into the school system as well as differing learning processes. This is also the case for many other school systems, most especially in the US. The key variables here include poverty, the literacy skills of parents as well as the parents' social network together with the overall level of financial investment in the school.

In Alberta, schools perform well on international measures of attainment, such as PISA and Trends in Mathematics and Science Study (TIMSS). However, when Provincial Achievement Test data are reviewed, significant differences exist between schools in terms of their performance on these standardized tests. Indeed, differences are so substantial, the Minister of Education dismissed a school board whose district (Northlands) had significant and sustained under-performance in comparison with others.

This is a complex challenge. Poverty and values, as well as social conditions and community, shape educational attainment and attitudes towards learning. The school is part of a complex system of interactions that shape learning and performance. Securing equity so that schools are a great learning place for all students requires new thinking, new approaches to teaching and learning, and new patterns of investment.

Equity in education has two dimensions. The first is fairness, which basically means making sure that personal and social circumstances – gender, socio-economic status or ethnic origin, for example – should not be an obstacle to achieving educational potential. The second dimension is inclusion, in other words, ensuring a basic minimum standard of education for all – for instance, that everyone should be able to read, write and complete simple arithmetic. The two dimensions are closely intertwined: tackling school failure helps to overcome the effects of social deprivation, which often causes school failure.

The OECD, which is increasingly seeing equity as the cornerstone of an educational strategy that countries need to adopt, suggests that there are 10 steps to achieve equity in education. These are:

In Designing an Education System Focused on Equity:

- Limit early tracking and streaming and postpone academic selection.

- Manage school choice so as to contain the risks to equity.

- In upper secondary (high school), provide attractive alternatives, remove dead ends and prevent drop-out.

- Offer second chances to gain from education.

For education practice:

- Identify and provide systematic help to those who fall behind at school and reduce year repetition.

- Strengthen the links between school and home so as to assist disadvantaged parents in helping their children to learn.

- Respond to diversity and provide for the successful inclusion of migrants and minorities within mainstream education.

Resourcing:

- Provide strong education for all, giving priority to early childhood provision and basic schooling.

- Direct resources to the students with the greatest need.

- Set concrete targets for more equity, particularly related to low school attainment and dropouts.

And, while Canada performs well on some of the OECD indicators of educational equity (better than Finland in mathematics and just behind Finland in reading); there is much to do to make equity the cornerstone of our thinking in relation to education and its future. If we do not, then the vendor-driven GERM ideology of education beckons.

Conclusion

The great baseball legend Yogi Berra once famously said "the future isn't what it used to be." He was right. We should take comfort, then, from Dan Quayle's belief that "the future will be better tomorrow." However, it will only be so if we address equity as the central challenge for Canada in the 21st century. How can we develop educational and social strategies that distinguish Canada as the most equitable of all of the developed nations? This is the challenge we should each address through our own work.

References

Canadian Council on Learning. (2011). *What is the Future of Learning in Canada?* Ottawa: Canadian Council on Learning available at http://www.ccl-cca.ca/pdfs/CEOCorner/2010-10-11WhatistheFutureofLearninginCanada.pdf

Dyke, L.S. and Duxbury, L.E. (2011). *The Implications of Subjective Career Success. Journal for Labour Market Research,* 43, 219-229.

Finkel, E. (November, 2012). Flipping the script in K12. District Administration (mimeo). Retrieved from www.districtadministration.com/article/flipping-script-k12

Flipped Learning Network. (2012). Improve student learning and teacher satisfaction with one flip of the classroom. Retrieved from author at http://flippedlearning1.files.wordpress.com/2012/07/classroomwindowinfographic7-12.pdf

Miner, R. (2012). *Jobs for the Future – Options and Opportunities.* Miner Consulting (mimeo). Available at http://abclifeliteracy.ca/files/Jobs_of_the_Future_Final.pdf

Murgatroyd, S. (2012). *Rethinking the Future – Six Patterns for the New Renaissance.* Edmonton, AB: *future*THINK Press.

OECD. (2013*). Education at a Glance.* Available online at http://www.oecd.org/edu/eag2013%20(eng)--FINAL%2020%20June%202013.pdf

Sahlberg, P. (2011). *Finnish Lessons – What Can the World Learn from Educational Change in Finland?* New York, NY: Teachers College Press.

UNESCO. (1996). *Learning – The Treasure Within* (Delors Report). Paris: UNESCO.

Chapter 2: The History of Alberta's Equity Journey – A 120 Year Story

Ernest C. Clintberg, EdD

Retired Associate Executive Secretary, Alberta Teachers' Association & Adjunct Professor, University of Alberta

Introduction

The historical journey of the Alberta government to advance the ephemeral goal of offering quality public equal educational opportunity to all (also known as equity) is the focus of this chapter. For the purpose of this chapter, public education is defined as education being provided for kindergarten to grade 12 students within school jurisdictions governed by publicly elected school trustees and publically funded. There are three distinct sections to this chapter (1) A history or review of equity covering 1880 to 1971; (2) a review of a 30-year period from 1971 to 2000; and (3) a quick review of the years from 2000 to 2013. This chapter, based on a doctoral research study initiated in 2005, offers both insights and further questions and opportunities for further analysis outlined in the author's end note.

It is a truism that equity may be reviewed from many perspectives. For the purposes of this chapter, three are considered: 1) equity for students; 2) fiscal equity for taxpayers; and 3) policy initiatives to establish, maintain and improve equity. To encapsulate these three perspectives three key points are worth noting:

1.	Efforts have been made in Alberta to establish and improve equity for students in public education from a variety of politicians, taxpayers, teachers and parents before and after the time of Canada's Confederation in 1867. Any success from these efforts has been, in a large part, because people established foundational policy that allowed the public education system to prosper and address issues around equity. It is the thesis of this chapter that because of these efforts in public education, private and charter school offerings have experienced only mild growth and have not taken traction in a significant way in the province.

2.	Fiscal equity, whether for students or for taxpayers, is an economic term that is attached to tax regimes to raise funds and revenue for school jurisdictions. However, fiscal equity may not define or meet the question of adequate funding and social justice delivery of an education that meets all student needs. This chapter, or the related research, does not deal with adequacy; neither does it deal with social justice, but both should be considered if one is to improve equal opportunity in public education. The research backing this chapter was done between 2000 and 2005, which led to the completion of a dissertation on the topic (Clintberg, 2005).

3.   Policy development has played a significant role in advancing equity in education, and this can be observed prior to An Ordinance Providing for the Organization of School in the North West Territories of 1884 with improvements made over the ensuing 125 years up to the current review of education called Inspiring Education.

It is the central conclusion of the chapter that Alberta's public education system has addressed the education of students with a growing understanding and application of equity in ways that have seen students' needs met by qualified teachers and accomplished with significant community support. While equity has improved, there still is the need for more thought and effort on equity and how it relates to the issue of adequate funding – the full realization of both remains elusive. Further, when funding for education has been reduced, equity has obviously been observed to be threatened as the discourse politicians moves from being 'student centred' to being 'tax or 'expenditure' centred.

It is important to recognize that the original research that began in 2005 chose to consider a 30-year time period and to ask the questions of politicians and civil servants who were engaged during this time because they were available for interviews. It would have proved to be interesting to gain the perspective of earlier legislators. But that was not possible; hence, the period chosen has been within the living memory of the researcher and those interviewed. Prior to 1971, the research depended solely on the written historical record. After 1971, coincidently the time that the Progressive Conservatives came to power, the research has had the opportunity to gain information through the interviewing of prominent players in public education, review documents that included Hansard, the official record of the proceedings of the Alberta Legislative Assembly.

A Review of Equity from 1880 to 1971

Equity for the taxpayer and the student in Alberta's education system is rooted in the time following Confederation in Canada and before the Province of Alberta was incorporated in 1905. Frank Oliver attended a meeting of prominent Edmonton citizens at a local hotel during January 1881 to discuss making it possible for all children in Edmonton, including Aboriginal children, to attend school without cost. Two years later Oliver introduced An Ordinance Providing for the Organization of Schools in the North West Territories in the Territories' council. This ordinance passed into law in 1884 and gave universal access to schooling in the Territories. Protestant and Roman Catholic school boards were allowed to establish schools and were granted powers to control and manage them through teacher certification, textbooks, and the inspection of schools. This may be described as limited "equal distribution," a level of equity characterized by Alexander (Alexander, 1982) in which all students who have a school available to them have equal and free access to education.

In 1901, the Legislative Assembly of the North West Territories passed an amendment to the school ordinance that required all students between the ages of six and 16 to attend school, and no fee was levied. However, school supplies were no longer free as they had previously been under the ordinance of 1884, but exceptions were made for those who could not afford the cost of textbooks and other supplies; the ordinance allowed school jurisdictions, where necessary, to waive these added expenses. Because school was mandatory only to age 16, school boards were allowed by statute to levy a set fee on students who attended from Standard V to high school. Equality of access was provided for in legislation up to Standard V. However, rural students were less likely to attend school than their urban counterparts were. In order to encourage rural students, the territorial government provided a more favourable funding level to rural school jurisdictions when their students attended school for a prescribed number of days.

In 1901, if Catholics formed a majority in an area, by statute their school was termed a public school jurisdiction. In those areas where they were a minority, Catholics could create a separate school jurisdiction with exactly the same privileges as the public school jurisdictions had. In this is found an equality of treatment under the law for school jurisdictions.

Measures were taken in the 1910s to cause funding to be equalized and encourage students to attend school. One of these amendments to the School Grants Ordinance in 1913 assured students who attended school from Standard V to the high school level of an education free of cost to them. Another was an amendment to the tax ordinance that provided equalization of educational opportunity when the government added more support through a special grant to the schools in poorer areas by compensating school jurisdictions with an assessment below $75,000. Taxpayers saw these measures as characteristic of restitution, as Alexander (Alexander, 1982) identified them, because remedial fiscal programs focused on weaknesses.

Special-needs students were offered programs in a limited way at the beginning of the 1900s. Edmonton received a grant to establish a school for "mentally defective children" in 1917. Calgary was the recipient of the first sight-saving class in Alberta through the government's provision of a grant of $875 in 1930 (Dent, 1956, p. 56).

In 1931, the provincial government (the ruling party was the United Farmers of Alberta) responded to the adverse conditions that farmers had faced in 1930 with an equalization grant to school jurisdictions where the ability of property taxpayers to pay sufficient taxes to cover the cost of education was hindered because of the assessed low valuation of property in the jurisdiction. This grant made it possible for a large number of school jurisdictions to continue to operate during these financially difficult times. In addition, the Tax and Rate Collection Act made the taxation procedure for education uniform amongst school jurisdictions, which improved fiscal equity amongst taxpayers and allowed schools to remain open, an effort of "equal distribution" (Swanson & King, 1997, p. 320).

In 1936, the provincial government (the ruling party was the Alberta Social Credit Party led by Premier William Aberhart) reorganized and consolidated rural school jurisdictions into larger units of administration. Consolidation in many instances improved the opportunity for students in rural Alberta to access a broader range of programming than they would have been able to do earlier. The economies of scale worked to their advantage, particularly at the high school level. By 1943 most rural school jurisdictions belonged to one of the 50 large school divisions. These consolidations may be considered a corrective program that resolved problems caused by the government's structure of school jurisdictions. Therefore, it can be characterized as an effort in improving "equal distribution" (Swanson & King, 1997, p. 320).

Gerhart, Minister of Education, announced in 1955 that grants for education would increase to cover 50% of the operation costs of elementary and secondary education. This measure was a precursor to the School Foundation Program Fund (SFPF). Its purpose was "to provide all schools with sufficient funds to achieve a basic minimum educational program, regardless of the fiscal ability they possessed" (Kulba, 1974, p. 118).

A Royal Commission on Education was established in 1957. The resulting report of what became known as the Cameron Commission (Province of Alberta. 1959) identified appropriate educational opportunity for all youth as a general concern. If a school jurisdiction was unable to finance such programs of equal opportunity, the commission recommended that the government fund the program. To improve the level of instruction for students across Alberta, the commission also recommended that, to gain a teaching certificate, teachers be required to have a Bachelor of Education degree. All these recommendations could have the potential to improve equity for students, if adopted.

The Foundation Program, which became known as the SFPF, was established in 1961, and proved to be a very significant step toward providing equal opportunity for students. The purpose of the SFPF was to offer a grant of equal value regardless of where the student attended school. The principles of the grant were that it would have an equalization factor between school jurisdictions, that the SFPF would raise local school revenues to a defined minimum level to cover essential services at current costs, that school jurisdictions would raise tax funds at a common mill rate, and that the balance of the foundation program would be secured with a provincial grant. This fund improved equal opportunity and equality for students while relieving taxpayers in poorer school jurisdictions of the burden of paying a disproportionate property tax compared to those in wealthier jurisdictions.

As a result, the recommendation from a Social Credit (Socred) government committee on school finance in 1969 fine-tuned the Foundation Program and changed the methods of funding school jurisdictions. The objective was to provide fiscal equalization (Alberta Department of Education, 1969a, p. 83). This was successful as long as the supplementary requisition levels of school jurisdictions remained low, but when these levels began to increase as a proportion of the total revenue collected for education, the objective of greater fiscal equalization began to be lost.

These initiatives and events spanning from 1880 to 1971 prepared the stage for the Progressive Conservative (PC) government's 1971 launch of another series of policies to achieve equitable treatment of students and taxpayers.

The Arrival of Progressive Conservative Era

Lou Hyndman, Minister of Education from 1971 to 1975, and the Department of Education officials who worked with him gained the support of the Alberta Legislature in addressing preschool and elementary education. They came to the task with a set of beliefs that included equity and fairness and had been influenced by a successful election campaign that recognized parents' and teachers' pleas that children with handicaps be part of the funded public school system. Hyndman believed that the preschool and elementary years were the most important in a child's education. He paid close attention to education in two areas, for handicapped children and for preschool children up to the sixth grade, which in his interview he called the formative years. As a result, frameworks were designed with specific program grants that supported and encouraged improved special-education programs and elementary educational opportunity for students. The frameworks included raising teacher certification standards by improving the level of teacher preparation for all teachers, not just for high school teachers who had previously been expected to have a degree. Now, all teachers were to have at least four years of university education.

Handicapped children in both institutions and special classrooms received additional attention through special funding grants to school boards to support such instruction and provide diagnostic tools for these students. In addition, Hyndman narrowed the gap in the factor of funding levels between elementary, junior high, and high school, which in effect raised the funding levels for elementary programs. Fiscal equity was further improved as the Department began to introduce an equalization grant to compensate school boards that had a poorer property tax base. To establish the Department's agenda and come to decisions about its concerns, Hyndman set in place a research arm in addition to consulting with the academic community and other stakeholders in education.

Julian Koziak (Minister of Education from 1975 to 1979) completed the work of narrowing the funding gap between elementary, junior high, and senior high school in 1976. He also introduced the equalization grant that Hyndman had proposed. Koziak established a growing number of grants to help offset the fiscal constraints of some of the poorer boards because of their low property assessment. He also improved fiscal equity for separate school districts when he allowed corporations to declare their taxes for either the public or the separate school district. In addition, he provided a method for separate school districts to more easily expand the boundaries of their districts and capture a wider tax base, thereby improving equitable funding. Koziak brought his experience as a lawyer to his position as minister: He focused on doing the best that he could for the client. His clients, both students and their parents, continued to influence him through MLAs in the Legislature. Individuals and groups brought concerns to the government, amongst them concerns about education. In the "golden era" when oil and gas royalties provided sufficient money to fund new programs, how could he refuse to address the concerns bought forward? Koziak asked (Clintberg, 2005, p.187).

David King (Minister of Education from 1979 to 1985) maintained the measures that had been established to provide equal educational opportunity and fiscal equity. Very early in his tenure as minister, King responded to the Carriere court decision, which established that handicapped students could attend their home school without impediment. As a result, the Department responded to school districts that complained that their lack of resources hindered their compliance. The Department improved the resources for handicapped students. In concert with the Canadian Constitution (1982) and the accompanying Canadian Bill of Rights (1985), the court's decision positively affected equity for the handicapped; however, it meant that educational costs increased. An Alberta Supreme Court decision, based on the Canadian Constitution, also improved francophone educational rights in 1983, and children were given the right to receive a francophone education. However, francophone education was limited to locations where there were a sufficient number of students. King began to review the School Act during his ministry, and the review resulted in a major revision in 1988. During Premier Lougheed's leadership, King said that Lougheed believed that everyone should be listened to and effectively heard; everyone had influence when it came to setting government agendas (Clintberg, 2005, p.342). This included the Opposition. Even though only four MLAs formed the Opposition during the years that King was minister, Hansard (Legislative Assembly of Alberta, 1979, 1980, 1981, 1982, 1983, 1984, 1985, 1986) suggested that they were heeded on issues related to education and equity. King prided himself on his effort to listen and debate education issues of the day with all stakeholders. Nine equity grants were created to deal with a variety of funding shortfalls that school boards faced. A number of them complained that these funds were complex and needed to be simplified. The grants were then rolled into a single equity grant in the same year that the government's grants to education were held to a 0% increase. The question arose as to whether the consolidation of the nine equity grants diminished equitable delivery of education or not. During King's tenure as minister, the phrase equal educational opportunity was replaced in political circles with the word equity.

Nancy Betkowski (Minister of Education from 1986 to 1989) brought beliefs that were similar to those of King to her position as minister. She avowed to meet with and listen to stakeholders in education (Clintberg, 2005, p.343). As a new mother, Betkowski viewed many of the issues through maternal eyes. This was most evident when she worked with her Department and the Legislature as she guided a major revision of the School Act through the Legislative Assembly. She believed that children must have the right to be treated equitably in their education and that this begins with having access to their local school. It is interesting that during the preparation for amendments to the School Act, she also attempted to bring the UN Rights of the Child to the attention of her caucus and sought their support, only to be turned down. In the Legislative Assembly she listened to all who spoke—government and opposition alike—to the issues for which she was responsible in education, and the School Act was amended based on the debate. This was also the case when the Department's budget was being debated in meetings of the Committee of Supply. Betkowski and Dinning, who followed her as minister, confirmed that under her direction the School Act focused on equity for students. To assure equity for all students, she believed that she needed to ensure that all students had access to an education regardless of where they lived and what their abilities or handicaps were.

In 1987, Betkowski was required to reduce funding to education by 3%, but she increased funding for special-needs students. She regretted that she had been unable to implement corporate pooling of taxation revenue despite her sincere efforts to do so. She and Bosetti saw corporate pooling as a way to address growing disparity between the poor and the wealthy school boards. Betkowski's efforts failed in caucus after difficult debates that tended to split the caucus, and those who opposed corporate pooling won the day. It is interesting that as early as 1987 MLA Halvar Jonson championed corporate pooling during the debate on the education estimates and implemented it in 1995. The mild and moderate grants for special-needs education were rolled into the SFPF; however, subsequent Ministers of Education reported them as the portion of the SFPF that this grant represented.

Jim Dinning (Minister of Education from 1988 to 1992) inherited the growing problem of fiscal equity amongst the school boards that was caused by a varied tax base, whether it was corporate or residential (Clintberg, 2005, p. 344). Dinning traveled with Department officials across the province to meet with school board trustees in an effort to reach consensus on models to resolve fiscal inequities amongst the boards. He was unsuccessful despite his attempts to hear all sides in the hope of achieving an acceptable compromise. The disparities continued to increase, and the importance of the types of research that had been conducted under Hyndman waned during Dinning's tenure. The MACOSF (Minster's Advisory Council on School Finance) had not met since 1981. By Dinning's time, research appears to have become governed more by politics and MLA committees than by empirical research. Instead of in depth and broad research, the Department's discussion papers began the rounds with Betkowski and continued with Dinning. These discussion papers tended to move into a more political-based decision-making model than the academic research model experienced previously up to the time MACOSF lost its place.

Halvar Jonson (Minister of Education from 1992 to 1996) inherited the fiscal equity problem when he became Minister of Education. A second problem, an annual deficit and the growing provincial debt, plagued the government throughout the 1990s and became an issue in a hotly contested party leadership campaign in which Klein defeated Betkowski. Klein became Premier and called an election in 1993, campaigning on a platform of eliminating the government's deficit and debt. Jonson was one of Klein's supporters in caucus; as Minister of Education appointed in 1992, he accepted the challenge to eliminate the deficit and debt. Jonson met with Treasury, which Dinning chaired, in 1993 and had the support of Bosetti in dealing with the fiscal equity issue. However, Bosetti opposed the proposed education budget cut of 20%; he did not see how school boards could continue to operate with such a severe cut to government funding. In the meeting the Treasury resolved the fiscal equity problem by implementing corporate pooling, taking over all taxing authority from the school boards, and implementing the new equalized assessment scheme. It was agreed that education would experience only a 12.6% cut to its budget. When the plan came into effect in 1995, property taxpayers in many cases experienced a drop in their tax bill for education (Clintberg, 2005, p. 344).

The Department also developed a new fiscal framework in 1994 that distributed funds in envelopes for instruction, facilities, transportation, and administration. A sparsity and distance grant continued to assist those school districts with higher costs because of their distances from major centres. High-needs students remained funded by the government; however, the grant was capped, which meant that there was no funding provided beyond a specified number of students. Therefore, these additional high-needs students did not qualify their school boards for the additional funding. ECS funding was cut by 50%, which left school boards with the option of reducing their program, charging tuition fees to keep it, or supplementing it with instructional money. Although equal funding at a reduced level from the previous year was provided for the regular student, the public and the Opposition raised another issue: adequacy. The Opposition questioned whether the new funding framework was equitable for students and school boards. Jonson and the government did not relent or respond to the repeated questions and demands in the Legislature, and the Opposition made no headway in the Legislature in changing the government's policy. Debt reduction drove the decision to pool all education tax sources; Jonson's and Dinning's resolve to fix the fiscal equity problem was successful according to those interviewed. On the other hand, the question of equity for students and adequacy remained during Minister Mar's tenure as the effects of a drop in funding for education, while some argued affected all students equally, did diminish equity for students with special needs, especially the measure to cap the funds for high-needs students (Clintberg, 2005, p. 345).

Gary Mar (Minister of Education from 1996 to 1999) maintained the Jonson funding framework. He sought no changes to it other than reinstating funding for ECS and removing the cap on high-needs funding. These measures were implemented following a review by an MLA team chaired by Wayne Jacques, a PC MLA. Research was completed as needed.

The Opposition continued to question the government on adequacy and equity for funding, to no avail. When Dr. Lyle Oberg took on the portfolio, which now included Advanced Education, the funding formula, with only the previously mentioned changes, remained the same other than for the annual percentage funding increases (Clintberg, 2005, p. 345).

Fiscal Equity and Equal Educational Opportunity from 1970-2000: What really changed?

Did the concept of fiscal equity evolve to address changing circumstances over the period of 1970 to 2000? From the research (Clintberg, 2005) it appears that the concept and its objectives for government policy did not change appreciably. However, the methods to achieve fiscal equity did change with the introduction of equity grants. In 1995 when Jonson was minister, the government took the authority to tax property away from the school boards and left them with access to tax only through plebiscite—a more significant change to fiscal equity. This method brought about the greatest degree of fiscal equity for the province in its history, according to all of those interviewed.

Equal educational opportunity or equity for students from the time of Hyndman until 2000 did change, in understanding, definition, and method of delivery. Initially, when the PCs were first elected and formed the government, equal educational opportunity was an objective for students who were seen as normal; others who did not meet this standard were placed in segregated programs, either in institutions or in special schools within the school district in which they lived. These students who were segregated in the "other" category had mental, vision, or hearing handicaps, and school districts saw little or no obligation to educate them. Late in the 1960s the need for services to those students, including education, became a more urgent issue for their parents, and they learned that their voices had been heard by Opposition PC MLAs. When the PCs formed the government in 1971, early items on the agenda included improving services in education for the handicapped and better defining the term learning-disabled students. The change in definition of the handicaps and the special-education needs changed under Hyndman's tenure as minister and was refined under other ministers. Children with handicaps had most often been segregated in an institutional setting. Not until the Carriere court decision in 1978 did the definition change to expect school boards to directly accept handicapped children into their home schools. This change was consistent with the Canadian Bill of Rights (1960) and later reinforced by the Canadian Constitution (1982). The School Act still did not acknowledge such rights of access in the early 1980s; not until 1988 did this element of right of access for students appear in the newly amended School Act tabled by Minister Betkowski. After the new School Act was declared law in 1988, children with handicaps gained the legislated right of access to regular classrooms. This demonstrated an evolution in the understanding, approach, and methods used to achieve equitable treatment of special-needs students from the time that Hyndman was appointed minister until 1999 when Oberg began his tenure. When Hyndman took responsibility for education, special-needs students were not funded other than through a limited opportunity fund and institutional programs. By 1999 these same students had access to funded programs that were often provided for in the regular classroom in their home schools.

The Key Influences on Equity 1970-2000

As the larger doctoral research study revealed (Clintberg, 2005) a number of factors resulted in changes to the definition of and the methods used to achieve fiscal equity and equal educational opportunity:

1.   The beliefs that individuals, elected or appointed to serve in the Department of Education, brought to their office:
       a.   Hyndman and Hawkesworth both believed that the preschool and elementary years were important and needed more resources, which led to a change in the funding ratio that increased elementary funding and introduced ECS.
       b.   A common belief of each minister was that children should have access to education, regardless of where they lived in Alberta or their circumstances. This belief gained Hyndman's attention and support, but was advanced when King initiated changes to the School Act. Betkowski completed the task of making access a legislated right when she guided Bill 27 through the Legislature in 1988.
       c.   Because of her strong beliefs in the rights of children, Betkowski accepted the UN Resolution on the Rights of the Child and promoted it (unsuccessfully) within caucus. Nonetheless, she guided a major revision to the School Act through 1987 and 1988. The new act focused on students and ensured access to an education.
2.   The circumstances that led to decisions and influenced the direction that the government took:

a. In 1970 and 1971 parents and teachers pressured the (Socred) government to improve services and access for children with handicaps. Instead of the Socreds' responding, the PC Opposition listened and developed policy based on what they heard. In part, that listening to parents and teachers likely contributed to their forming the government because they responded to the demands.

b. Jonson and the government addressed fiscal equity in 1995 based on a prolonged debate to resolve the fiscal disparities amongst school districts. With the government seeking to reduce deficits and debt, Jonson as Minister of Education and Dinning as Provincial Treasurer acted to equalize funding by taking over the responsibility for collecting property and corporate taxes for education. If that had not happened, the reductions in government funding to education might have severely crippled the poorest school districts.

3. The court decisions, the Canadian Constitution, and the Canadian Bill of Rights that influenced government responses:

a. The Carriere court decision influenced the direction that the government took in funding and providing opportunity for all students, regardless of their handicap, to attend their home school. This decision appears to have ensured that handicapped children would be integrated into their home school.

b. Further, the Canadian Constitution of 1982 contributed to ensuring that children with handicaps are included in regular classrooms as a norm rather than as an exception.

c. Francophone education was advanced because parents challenged the government through the courts under the Charter of Rights and Freedoms. When the court decided in their favour, parents won the right for their children to be educated in a francophone school.

d. Nine school boards challenged the government through the courts, alleging that the funding framework of 1993 caused severe fiscal inequities that disadvantaged poorer school jurisdictions in relation to wealthier jurisdictions. The court case never made it to a full hearing because the court deemed that the nine school boards lacked jurisdiction to make a complaint. The challenge may have influenced Jonson, the minister, and Bosetti, the deputy minister, in the measures that they took to Treasury in the fall of 1993 when the initial decisions to change the funding structures for education were made. These structural changes included the move in 1994-1995 to take over both property and corporate education taxes and to pool them into the ASFF for equal distribution.

4.   Research and the political process that influenced the Department's decisions (Figure below illustrates this change in influence):

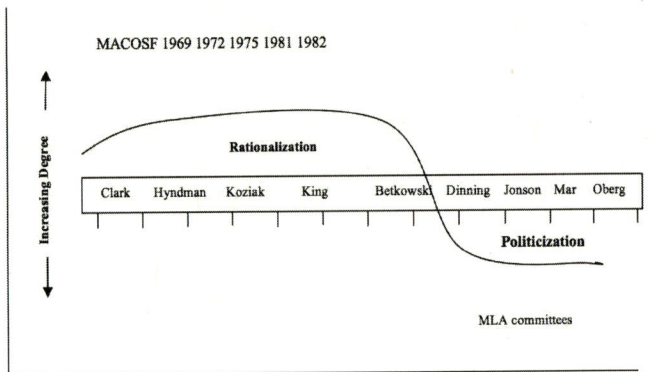

Figure 5: Attention to the approach to decision making.

- Hyndman began a period of rationalization when he budgeted for research activity. Hyndman also continued Clark's earlier practice of establishing an advisory group to the minister made up of stakeholders and academics. The reliance on empirical research continued into the mid 1980s; the MACOSF met and delivered reports in 1969, 1972, 1975, 1981, and 1982.

- As the emphasis on empirical research waned, as shown in Figure 5, and the Minister's Advisory Committee was disbanded. It appears that the process of decision making within the Department became more politicized in the early 1990s. Roundtables on education in 1993 and the Jacques Committee that studied equity in education in 1995 and again in 1999 were examples of politicization because they involved politicians and the public rather than empirical research. The new research from Dinning's tenure forward was conducted to make spot checks, such as Sloan's request that Wiebe determine whether high-needs funding was effective and deserved to have the cap removed on funding.

- Prior to the PC government, the legislative debate and delegations to cabinet and the legislative debate had influence on the Socred government. The influence shifted to caucus, the Legislative debate, individual MLAs, and the Opposition during the tenures of Hyndman, Koziak, King, and Betkowski. These groups had considerably less influence on Dinning, Jonson, and Mar. Often in Hansard the first four ministers listed above received suggestions from the floor of the Legislature during debate and question period. Jonson and Mar, on the other hand, appeared defensive to Opposition questions about the government's direction, following Klein's announcement in his January 1993 televised broadcast that the government's deficit and debt needed to be reduced. He therefore advised cuts to all departments, including education. Figure 6 illustrates the changes in Legislature influence.

- The emphasis on the 1970 fiscal equity concerns under Clark seems to have changed to an emphasis on equal educational opportunity under Hyndman. This was followed by a long period of interest in equal educational opportunity, or student equity as King described it, until the late 1980s, when Betkowski's attention shifted to corporate pooling. Because of the provincial debt, fiscal equity gained attention in the early 1990s under Dinning. By 1993 fiscal equity gained further prominence.

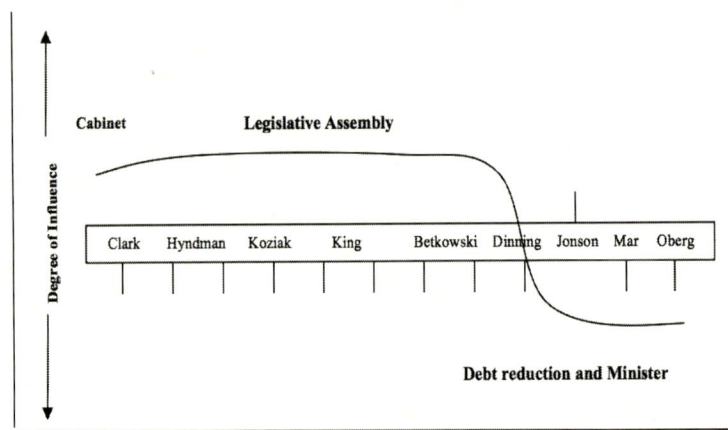

Figure 6: Influence of the Legislative Assembly vs. The Government

This was apparent when Jonson and Bosetti met with the Treasury, chaired by Dinning, and decided that the government would take over property taxing authority from school boards. Although each Minister may be seen as having dealt with both sides of the equity equation—fiscal equity and equal educational opportunity—the evidence suggests that the emphasis shifted from one element of equity to the other quite deliberately in response to the political environment and what each minister saw as most important at the time that he or she was in office. Figure 7 illustrates the shift in emphasis between the two elements; however, during the tenure of each minister each side of the equation did receive some attention.

At the close of the period from 1970 to 2000, the general question raised in the larger research study was, "Did fiscal equity and equal educational opportunity improve?" The information from the interviews and other data that I collected suggested that fiscal equity improved dramatically in 1995 when ratepayers gained greater equity and school boards were funded more equitably under the ASFF. However, in 1995 the school jurisdictions that had become used to the extras that their wealthier tax bases provided were affected by the government's new framework for tax collection and equalization of revenue to school districts. In turn, after 1995 these property tax funds went into the ASFF and were redistributed equally to all school districts across the province.

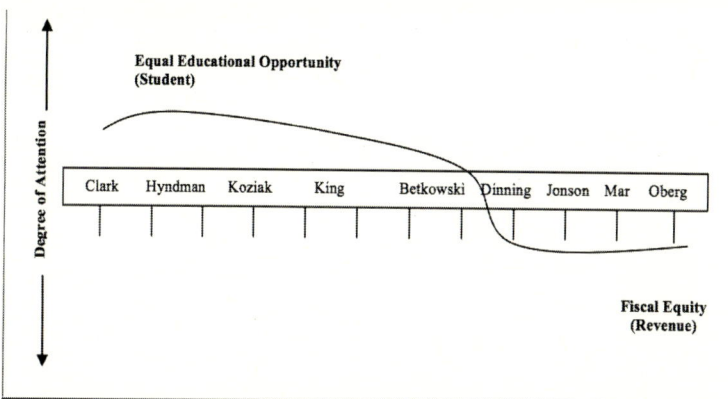

Figure 7: Attention given to the elements of equal educational opportunity and fiscal equity.

Prior to 1995, poorer school boards may have had less demand from parents for student education services than wealthier boards had. In 1995, with the new funding structure, the poorer boards supported the new funding formula that boosted their funding, and the previously wealthier boards lost revenue. Some of the previously wealthy school boards complained that the significant shortfall in funding under the new framework of 1995 caused their school systems to suffer. Although it focused on equalized funding, some, including Tom Olson from Parkland SD in a report he had prepared (Olson, 1999), argued that some of the main cost drivers such as the average cost of teachers, which was not a consideration in the funding framework after 1995, needed to be addressed to achieve full fiscal equity. Increasing facility costs, deteriorating school buildings, and the need for new schools have not been met adequately with funding from the government since 1995. However, Wiebe claimed that it was this shortfall in fiscal equity in the new funding formula that required attention, not the cost drivers that Olson had mentioned.

Fiscal equity tools, as Hyndman described them, are blunt instruments for funding education and addressing all of its complexities. This problem added to that of the block funding that was initiated in 1984 with equity grants being rolled into one, followed by the enveloped (block) funding used in all of the revenue streams to school boards from 1995 until 2003. It can be argued that block funds make fiscal equity tools even blunter and less flexible in meeting the variable costs of delivering education. With few funds to address the variability with sparsity and distance, transportation, and special high-needs funding, there is not sufficient latitude to address the complexities of delivering equal educational opportunity to students wherever they live and whatever their circumstances.

The original research referred to a review of history dating back before Confederation (1867) and focused on a thirty year span from 1970 to 2000; however, since then until 2013 Alberta has experienced discussion and policy development that may be seen to affect equity for students, mainly around the topic of inclusion of special needs students. However, for the Alberta taxpayer, there have not been any changes from those observed prior to 2000. In 2004, during Lyle Oberg's (Minister of Education from 1999 to 2004) watch, the funding framework for a student changed and became more complex: It acknowledged factors, not only of distance from major centres, but also of economic and educational needs of Aboriginal students. The amended framework was not within the scope of the original research study; however, school boards argued that the funding the government promised was not as rich as it appeared to be; therefore, not as effective as hoped.

Following Oberg, Gene Zwozdesky (Minister of Education from 2004 to 2006), Ron Liepert (Minister of Education from 2006 to 2008) along with their Deputy Ministers managed the Department without any impact on equity.

From Inspiring Education to Fiscal Restraint: The Promise and Paradox of the Current Period

Dave Hancock (Minister of Education from 2008 to 2011) understood and articulated a need to improve equity for students. He initiated a examination of the education system by introducing a comprehensive review called Inspiring Education, followed an effort called transforming education (Alberta Education, 2011) to reform the education system. Within the report, prepared for Dave Hancock, values are addressed in a manner that acknowledges aspirations of equity and fairness for all students, where it states:

> Values are the beliefs and ideals we consider critical as we make decisions about education. Albertans expressed a desire for an education system rooted in these values: opportunity, fairness, citizenship, choice, diversity, and excellence. These values must be

embraced by all who comprise the learning community: learners, parents, families, educators, support staff, governors, and a diverse group of stakeholders which includes taxpayers. They must be reflected in every decision related to curriculum, teaching, assessment, policy and governance. The six core values, affirmed in community discussions, underpin the 3E's of education - Engaged Thinker, Ethical Citizen and Entrepreneurial Citizen (Alberta Education, 2010, p. 6-7). The values apply to every learner, including those who are urban, rural, Aboriginal, disabled, gifted, and of minority cultures (Alberta Education, 2010, p. 20).

The report goes on to use the language that favours equity in that the goal is to provide "Opportunity" such that "Learners are exposed to rich learning experiences that enable them to discover their passions and achieve their highest potential" and Fairness" where "Learners have access to the programs, support services, and instructional excellence needed to achieve desired outcomes where "Diversity" is addressed by "Learners' differing needs, cultures, and abilities are respected and valued within inclusive learning environments" (Alberta Education, 2010, p. 20-21). These are all aspirational, and there is hope these goals will be accomplished.

The efforts to transform public education, following the *Inspiring Education* report, has met with some challenges, which include how these efforts may be funded and what policy initiatives may be needed to match the aspirations of Alberta Education. One of the aspirations that may improve equity for students is to encourage student inclusion and the reports states:

> Every learner should have fair and reasonable access to educational opportunities regardless of ability, economic circumstance, location, or cultural background. Their needs and ways of life should be respected and valued within an inclusive learning environment. Some learners will require additional, specialized supports to fully access these opportunities (Alberta Education, 2010, p. 32).

This aspiration is something that was well established and operating in most school jurisdictions well prior to the report. However, some would argue that efforts of inclusion are not well funded and resources lacking to adequately address the needs of special needs students in a regular classroom now with expectations of full inclusion.

In summary, looking at the aspirations of the report *Inspiring Education,* it is difficult to see how they may come to fruition in the fiscally tight government environment of the 2013 Provincial Budget that seeks efficiencies and reductions. Jeff Johnson, Minister of Education, said of education in the 2013 budget that "… the fiscal reality is that many school boards will see fewer operating dollars this year compared to last year, and we will all need to work together to make sure kids aren't impacted in a negative way (Alberta Government, 2013)." This is a budget that effectively reduced the resources in classrooms due to the austerity measures taken across all levels of government, including education. Seeking efficiencies, from a policy perspective, typically works against any effort to promote equity and inclusion within the school system.

Hancock began a review of the School Act which resulted in a Bill being introduced into the Legislative Assembly in 2010, but this never came close to a final vote by the legislative assembly while he was minister. Thomas Lukaszuk (Minister of Education 2011) also made an effort to make these revisions to the School Act into a new statute, The Education Act, but it was not until after Jeff Johnson (Minister of Education from 2011 to the present) was appointed that the revisions gained Royal Assent, and the new act will likely be proclaimed in 2014, after the accompanying regulations are written. However, the revisions will not change the focus on equal access for students that Betkowski's efforts to revise the School Act (1988) did nor will it do much to improve on the equity for students in the education system.

Hancock had set out to accomplish a unification of effort to coordinate and improve the stead of children supported by Departments in government that deal with children, including the Alberta Education. These efforts are ongoing, and there is hope that they will result in better ways to support children in their access to education and other services in a coordinated and unified manner. This, when done, could be seen as an effort to cause equity to improve for children, along with other societal opportunities to address these children's growth and needs. It is yet to be seen if current efforts to transform education bring any change to improving equal opportunity for students.

Conclusion: Equity Achieved in This Decade?

The fundamental issue that has not been addressed is that of the adequacy of funding required in order to achieve the goal of a great school for all. While too obvious to state, it bears repeating that although funding frameworks may be fiscally equitable as determined by formulas, they may not provide sufficient funding on the ground to meet the educational needs of students adequately. So the seemingly new questions emerge that reflect long-standing public policy challenges in this province. Is there sufficient understanding of what the objectives of education entail to foster a clear understanding of what it will cost, and from that to determine whether funding is adequate? Will the provincial government consider equal opportunity for students within a social justice context rather than an economic context referenced in the Department's Alberta Education action agenda 2011-2014 (Alberta Education, 2011)? Will the effort to involve Aboriginal People and address their educational issues, found in the "action agenda" truly take into consideration the social justice issues and questions about funding adequacy to improve a very complex system for delivering education which needs a cooperative effort on the part of the provincial and federal Government?

Currently, there is an obvious disconnect between the cost of Alberta's having the highest paid teachers in Canada and the government's funding being in the mid-range of all of the other provinces' levels. The costs of educating students vary, possibly just as the cost of living varies across Alberta from small rural towns to cities that are experiencing economic booms. What are the implications for the funding framework if these factors are taken into consideration? How does the education funding framework avoid fuelling inflation in these various geographic centres?

Does the concept of equity for students need to be broadened to avoid the limitations of the current definition of equal educational opportunity? Are there new ways to view equity that are not limited by the available funding, or is the available funding what defines equity?

Historically, the literature, it can be argued, provides evidence that the concept of educational fiscal equity in Alberta was founded in the legislative decisions beginning with the British North America Act of 1867 and followed by the North West Territories Council's school ordinance of 1884. A thread of what can be described as educational fiscal equity appeared subsequent to the school ordinance of 1901, which subsequently was adopted in Alberta in 1905; it ensured that all school age children could attend school without cost, such as school fees and materials. In the event that ratepayers were unable to pay their taxes, school boards could waive their tax payment and allow the children of such ratepayers to attend school. In the early 1900s, schools for the deaf, deaf mutes, and the blind were established. From 1905 into the 1960s attempts to improve school attendance and the qualifications of teachers in rural areas also helped to establish a uniform delivery of educational programs and services to every student throughout Alberta. Where the programs were not available because of the lack of teachers and local resources, tuition agreements between school jurisdictions allowed students to attend school in other jurisdictions as non-residents and therefore to have access to programs not available to them locally. All of these attempts, however effective or discriminatory, show a real effort to establish the foundation for what is known today as educational fiscal equity.

The concept of educational fiscal equity has evolved over time, beginning in the 1880s with equal opportunity; apparently, this concept grew out of a sense of egalitarianism, a principle of equal rights and opportunity for all (Allen, 1990, p. 375). The evolution continued through to fiscal equality for both students and taxpayers in the mid-1900s. Finally, the concept of educational fiscal equity was introduced in the Alberta, then the North West Territories, education scene in the 1880s. The effort on the part of the Alberta government has demonstrated a desire to seek equitable treatment for all children of school age in Alberta.

Equity for students, whether fiscal or educational opportunity, was discussed from three different perspectives in three arenas: the theoretical, which was addressed in the literature reviewed in the original research; the practical, mainly in the interviews with the government officials; and the political, in Hansard and the interviews with the Ministers of Education. The politicians often used the word equity to describe and promote programs—for example, EOF—amalgamation, and the elimination of non-operating school boards. Department officials more often referred to the theoretical approaches to equity discussed in the literature and did not see the three examples as efforts to achieve equity. In the formation of policy, one may conclude that equity is a word that flags fairness and is looked on favourably by the electorate; hence, politicians may use the word in a broad sense, outside the realm of the theoretical, to gain public support for their initiatives.

What does the future hold for educational fiscal equity and equal educational opportunity in Alberta? It is likely that the future will be based on characteristics related to the foundations that have been established and have evolved over the last 129 years with a steady advancement of the concepts. It is hoped that this discussion and any new research will add to that understanding and provide some direction for future decisions to improve educational fiscal equity and equal educational opportunity even more.

Although fiscal equity may be the first approximation of equal educational opportunity (MACOSF, 1975, p. 5), the government needs to continue to focus its attention not only on the fiscal side of the equation, but also on the equal educational opportunity side. Student success relies on adequate funding that is finely tuned to the needs of students, regardless of ability, social, or economic situation. Complex needs demand a more complex approach to defining the needs of students in school. Complex needs may require the broadening of funding frameworks to include more aspects of students' lives than simply what happens in the classroom and their scores on standardized tests. Last, the variable cost drivers of which Olson (Olson, 1999) spoke need to be looked at and funding designed to offset these costs in a fair and equitable fashion. Further, consideration should be given to other factors than just economic and include social justice issues related to adequate funding as part of the formula that makes up solutions addressing equal educational opportunity for students.

In closing, currently within neither the aspirations of Inspiring Education and efforts to transform education nor in the newly revised Education Act of 2012 (yet to be proclaimed) do we see anything that would significantly improve equity for the student or the taxpayer without considering new revenue and a tax regime that would address funding concerns. These hopes to improve equity appear to be taking steps backward as the education system effectively undergoes diminished funding and resources going forward into the 2013/2014 school year. Let us hope that looking forward over the next decades that the current aspirations for equity will find a foothold in the province and the resources needed for this will be realized.

References

Alberta Department of Education. (1969). *Education: The sixty-fourth annual report*. Edmonton, AB: Government of Alberta.

Alberta Education. (2010). *Inspiring Education: A Dialogue with Albertans*. Alberta Government, April 2010, Edmonton, AB: Government of Alberta.

Alberta Education. (2011). *Alberta Education Action Agenda* 2011-2014; 2011, Edmonton, AB: Government of Alberta.

Alberta Government. Building Alberta: Budget 2013 keeps the focus on students. News Release, March 7, 2013. http://alberta.ca/acn/201303/3378046B3A890-A09D-D222-DB9B59897D97B1AF.html

Alexander, K. (1982). *Concepts of equity*. In W. McMahon & T. Geske (Eds.), *Financing education: Overcoming inefficiency and inequality* (pp. 193-214). Urbana: University of Illinois Press.

Allen, R.E. (Eds.). (1990). The concise Oxford dictionary of current English (8th ed.). Oxford, UK: Clarendon Press.

British Parliament. British North America Act. 1867, London, Government of Alberta.

Clintberg, Ernest C. (1970 to 2000). *Changing Understandings of Equity: Alberta's Funding of Public Education*. 2005, University of Alberta, Edmonton, Government of Alberta.

Dent, I.G. (1956). *The evolution of school grants in Alberta*. Unpublished master's thesis, University of Alberta, Edmonton, AB.

Government of Canada. The Canadian Constitution. 1982, Government of Alberta.

Government of Canada. The Canadian Bill of Rights. 1986, Government of Alberta.

Kulba, J.W. (1974). *Equity in taxation and school finance: A relationship between property and income bases in Alberta census regions.* Eugene, OR: University of Oregon.

Legislative Assembly of Alberta. (1979). Alberta Hansard: The 19th legislature first session. Edmonton, AB: Queen's Printer.

Legislative Assembly of Alberta. (1980). Alberta Hansard: The 19th legislature second session. Edmonton, AB: Queen's Printer.

Legislative Assembly of Alberta. (1981). Alberta Hansard: The 19th legislature third session. Edmonton, AB: Queen's Printer.

Legislative Assembly of Alberta. (1982). Alberta Hansard: The 19th legislature fourth session. Edmonton, AB: Queen's Printer.

Legislative Assembly of Alberta. (1983). Alberta Hansard: The 20th legislature first session. Edmonton, AB: Queen's Printer.

Legislative Assembly of Alberta. (1984). Alberta Hansard: The 20th legislature second session. Edmonton, AB: Queen's Printer.

Legislative Assembly of Alberta. (1985). Alberta Hansard: The 20th legislature third session. Edmonton, AB: Queen's Printer.

Legislative Assembly of Alberta. (1986). Alberta Hansard: The 21st legislature first session. Edmonton, AB: Queen's Printer.

Legislative Assembly of Alberta. (1988). The School Act (1988). Edmonton, AB: Government of Alberta.

Legislative Assembly of Alberta. The Education Act (2012). December 12, 2012, Edmonton, AB: Government of Alberta.

MACOSF. (1975). The Minister's Advisory Committee on School Finance. Edmonton, AB: Government of Alberta.

Province of Alberta. (1959). Report of the Royal Commission on Education. Edmonton, AB: Government of Alberta.

Olson, T. (1999). Equity issues: Instructional block: A report to the Committee to Review the Funding Framework for School Boards. Edmonton, AB: Alberta Education.

Swanson, A.D., & King, R.A. (1997). *School Finance: Its Economics and Politics* (2nd ed.). New York, NY: Longman.

Chapter 3: Inclusion and Confusion in Alberta [1]

Chris Gilham, PhD, Faculty of Education, *St. Francis Xavier University* and

John Williamson, PhD candidate, Graduate Programs in Education, *The University of Calgary*

Introduction

Over the past 20 years (Winzer, 2009), the concept of inclusion has become ubiquitous in discussions about programming for students with diagnosed medical disabilities and other "exceptionalities" in public schooling throughout the Western world (Graham & Slee, 2008, Winzer, 2009, Gabel & Danforth, 2008). Critics note that while discussions about inclusion are often framed in opposition to or in tension with what has traditionally been called special education, they often are taken up within special educational structures and policies (Graham & Slee, 2008).

Institutional communications about inclusive education in policy papers, Minister's statements, website updates, and promotional videos recently released by Alberta Education (2009; 2012) for example, label inclusion as social progress beyond special education, and yet continue to seem derivative of special education thought and policy. In order to help inclusive education projects retain some of the activism that characterized earlier discourse about inclusive education, scholars have encouraged critical readings of the claims made by educational ministries, school districts, and individual educational institutions regarding inclusive educational practices (Graham & Slee, 2005; 2008; Valle and Connor, 2011; Thomas and Loxley, 2007). In similar spirit, this paper attempts to understand Alberta's seemingly confusing positions on inclusion by asking questions both of what was and is currently publicly available on the topic. The primary question this paper asks is: what remains concealed or at play beneath the glare of the recent shift from *Action on Inclusion* to *Diversity?*

---

[1] Materials in this chapter are based on: Gilham, C., & Williamson, W. J. (2013). Inclusion's confusion in Alberta. International *Journal of Inclusive Education*, 1-14. DOI: 10.1080/13603116.2013.802025 with acknowledgements.

Our Position

We support an inclusive education system. An inclusive education system would be a reformed school system (Skrtic, 1995; Slee, 2011), and special education would no longer retain its status as a parallel and competing educational system to "regular" education (Skrtic, 1995). We believe that the medical model of disability supports the parallel system, and as a consequence, often works as an obstacle to an inclusive education system.

Currently, Alberta's inclusive education program rests upon the medical model of disability, creating several challenges. This model can be pernicious because it stigmatizes labeled students as abnormal, subnormal or bearing deficits (Gilham, 2012; Goffman, 1963; Hacking, 2004; Nussbaum, 2006). This segregation of perceived normal and abnormal is perpetuated through the categorization of students into disabilities via the American Psychiatric Association's Diagnostic and Statistical Manual (DSM).

Furthermore, the medical model's notion of disability often encloses student differences as problems inherent to the student, which conceals larger systemic issues inherent to an industrial and antiquated model of education (Gilham, 2012; Jardine, 2013). Albertans also support the move away from "addressing disability as a problem" (Alberta, 2009a, p. 3). For example, 71% of study respondents claim to support replacement of disability-based coding and labeling with the identification of learning supports (p. 6).

We currently examine Alberta's inclusive education policy through a lens of concerned and cautious hope. We continue to look for and to track recent changes to what was once called "special education" in the province with the hope that a truly inclusive education system might arise. At the same time, we do not accept the policies, structures and practices of Alberta Education without questioning the historical influences that shape them. We do not take special education or its various instantiations (Exceptional Learners, Inclusive Education, etc.) for granted, nor do we accept that inclusion as special education is simply "the way things are".

Our position is not intended to "throw the baby out with the bathwater", however. We have successfully applied practices drawn from the traditional special education field, and we believe that certain students, labeled disabled or not, benefit from unique and particular educational practices. This understanding illuminates the diversity of human life and knowledge – not its disabilities. Along with other disability studies scholars, we believe that disability is a result of the conditions a culture can impose on particular people or, in this case, students (Reindal, 2009).

We do, however, acknowledge that human beings have impairments that clearly impact everyday activities (Reindal, 2009). We also believe that as a self-identified democratic society, we have both an ethical obligation to support the participation of all public citizens and a practical interest in enjoying the combined contributions of an inclusive environment. In our opinion, the overarching process of student codification and placement into segregated settings is often antithetical to these principles.

Alberta Education's Economical Move Towards Inclusion

In the fall of 2007, Alberta Education commissioned a review of "severe disability profiles." At the time, more than 16,000 students were designated as having "severe disabilities" (Alberta Education, 2008). From 2001-2002 until the 2012-2013 school year, students identified with a severe disability were assigned provincial dollars, separate from instructional block funding. Traditionally, block funding is applied to both basic instructional costs and supports for mild/moderate categories of disability (Jahnukainen, 2011). In 2011-2012, school boards received a $16,645 funding grant for each student labeled with a severe disability. Though ultimately free to apply that money however deemed appropriate, school boards were also required to annually document whether severely-coded students received of a range of specialized (and costly) services that included specialized assessment; a 2-students-to-1-adult ratio (teacher or teaching assistant) for significant portions of the day; specialized equipment or assistive technology; assistance with basic care; frequent documentation of medical and/or behaviour status and/or direct support services at a cost to the system (behaviour specialist, orientation and mobility specialist, etc.). (Alberta Education, 2011).

Throughout the past 20 years, there have been considerable increases in identification of students with severe disabilities. According to Winzer (2011):

> The period between 1998 to 2003 saw an increase of 64% in identification of students with severe disabilities and an increase of 140% for students with mild/moderate disabilities, compared to a general increase in the school population of 5% (p. 51).

The correlation between the rise in students with a severe disability designation and the subsequent funding in Western school jurisdictions has been described as "the bounty phenomenon" (Graham and Jahnukainen, 2011).

The bounty phenomenon is the only mechanism through which schools and school boards can acquire additional funds to support students. When school administrators are faced with exceptional student needs, they can either work through those challenges within the limits of their school means or they can start the referral process for student assessment, which often results in additional funding. This leads to ever-increasing demands on school psychologists to spend time on assessments when they could be working in classrooms alongside teachers and other support staff on behalf of students.

In turn, the need for school psychologists to complete assessments puts additional strain on school board resources. In an odd move of inversion, the bounty phenomenon perpetuates the student disablement, in effect, producing a variety of systemic sicknesses, which leads to increasing numbers of students labeled as severely disabled, an emphasis on diagnosis over support on the part of district-employed specialists (Specht, 2013), and a pervasive emphasis on the ways in which so many students are "sick" and are thereby in need of special education's best practices. This complex series of cascading consequences reinforces the need for a parallel and often separate special education system for the "abnormal", which runs counter to the democratic intent of inclusive education. Ivan Illich (1926-2002) described this cyclical process of ever-increasing disability as a result of the application or introduction of a perceived treatment or antidote as iatrogenesis (1976).

The 2007 severe disability profile review (Alberta Education, 2008) required that school boards produce documentation to justify the codification of students or to meet the burden of proof that all of severe-coded students qualified for funding. The province wanted to determine if school boards were consistently conforming to provincial policy. Criteria included an updated or current and appropriate diagnosis by qualified personnel; descriptions of how the disability affects or impacts a student in the learning environment; and identification of the types and intensity of supports provided to students (Alberta Education, 2008, p. 5). The review found that 48% of the files submitted did not conform to Alberta Education's criteria. As stated in the 2008 report:

> The review results suggest that there is inconsistent application of special education severe disabilities coding criteria across the province which raises questions about the interpretation and application of mild and moderate coding [as well]. Given the magnitude of these concerns, the results of the severe disabilities profile review are a catalyst for thorough examination of the overall special education framework (2008, p. 1).

We believe this review was the impetus for Alberta Education's publicly-driven inquiry into special education in the province, known as *Setting the Direction*. Less than a year after the review was completed, Alberta Education announced the establishment of working groups to propose policy. Province-wide consultations were initiated with various stakeholders to discuss reforms to special education. In a short video message, the then Minister of Education, David Hancock, promised that the reform would include "the development of policy, accountability measures and a funding mechanism" (Alberta Education, 2009).

While the *Setting the Direction* documentation (Alberta Education, 2009) speaks extensively to the need for the reformed system to support all students inclusively, the above statement from Hancock suggested that economic factors figured prominently into initiating the process. The bounty phenomenon's ever-increasing consequences, the subsequent Alberta Education review and the proposed policy reform all spoke to a parallel economic crisis surrounding the resources needed to appropriately support effective student learning.

Even as the *Setting the Direction / Action on Inclusion* rhetoric discussed how to improve inclusion for students with disabilities and thereby reduce their marginalization as abnormal "others", the issue of how to best manage the economic cost of these "others" remained, in ironic prominence, at the heart of policy making.

This has been an issue for Alberta's governments since its inception in 1905 as a province of Canada (ATA, 1999; Dechant, 2006).

The *Setting the Direction* consultations were broad and deep. The project resulted in a set of reform recommendations known as *Action on Inclusion*. *Action on Inclusion* spoke to a fundamental ethical shift in Alberta's classrooms. Key examples of the recommendations included:

- Moving from tolerating difference to valuing diversity.

- Moving from special education founded on a medical model based on the student's diagnosis to [a practice] of understanding a student's strengths and needs through [collaboration] in which teachers, parents, students and specialists…identify supports and services that best match the student's strengths and needs (Alberta, June 2009).

Perhaps most importantly, *Action on Inclusion* was driven by this promising definition of inclusion:

> *One inclusive education system where each student is successful.* Inclusive education system: a way of thinking and acting that demonstrates

universal acceptance of, and belonging for, all students. Inclusive education in Alberta means a value-based approach to accepting responsibility for all students. It also means that all students will have equitable opportunity to be included in the typical learning environment or program of choice (Alberta, June 2009).

The key factor in the above definition was: the ability for all students to have access to equitable opportunities and be included in a typical learning environment or program of choice. This statement hinted of the possibility that we would begin to see specialized settings and streamed course offerings, determined by coding/disability status and/or IQ score, as inequitable or unjust, and as sites and places of historical traditions that speak of marginalization and segregation (Dechant, 2006), despite our beliefs that we have been caring for such student through the deficit model of disability.

To Include or Not to Include

In 2011-2012, a number of confusing changes occurred on the website Alberta Education maintained to explain inclusive education reform - and the scope of the inclusion project was profoundly altered. In the spring of 2012, the *Action on Inclusion* website and the *Setting the Direction* materials were removed and replaced with this short statement: *Action on Inclusion* no longer exists as a project or initiative, but the work continues as part of our collective practice to build an inclusive education system in Alberta (Alberta Education, 2012, para. 4).

Months later, the *Action on Inclusion* web pages, policy statements and supporting resources were re-posted in the archives, along with a definition of inclusion that resembled the definition used during the reform period in 2009, notwithstanding a small but important change in adjectives. The 2009 definition promised to engage students in "typical learning environments and programs of choice." However, in the most recent (2012) definition, "typical" was changed to "appropriate learning environments". Currently:

> The goal of an inclusive education system is to provide all students with the most appropriate learning environments and opportunities

for them to best achieve their potential. Some have said this is what should already be happening in education, and they're right. However, some children, youth, and their families do not feel that they have the same opportunities as their peers.

In Alberta, inclusion in the education system is about ensuring that each student belongs and receives a quality education no matter their ability, disability, language, cultural background, gender, or age (Alberta, 2012a).

The above definition change returns us to original special education policy, which hinges on the notion of 'Least Restrictive Environments - LRE' (Kauffman, Crockett, Gerber, & Landrum, (2007). This traditional special education legislation permits students to be placed in different settings at the discretion of school boards, which is usually based on student difference as pathology or disability. We are concerned that the continued support of the LRE policy, clearly supported in the newest and current definition of inclusion, is the continuation of traditional practices of the segregation and integration of students into an unchanged school system. We wonder if Alberta Education has, for reasons we do not yet know, returned to its previous special education structure but continues to publicly say substantial changes to special education have been and will continue to be made.

Diversity's Messaging

Currently, under the title of *Inclusive Education,* one can find a short video on diversity as well as links to past projects and other related information. We think *Diversity in Alberta's Schools: A Journey to Inclusion* (Alberta Education, 2012) points to Alberta Education's misleading self-presentation noted above. Near the start of the video, the then Minister of Education says, "When you are looking at becoming an inclusive society, there really isn't a beginning or an end. It is all about a process. It is all about becoming accepting and inclusive and not reaching a finite goal." Despite this process-oriented message, the video seems to be strong evidence of the observations of Slee and Allan (2001) that "[w]e are still citing inclusion as our goal, still waiting to include, yet speaking as if we are already inclusive"

(p. 181), as well as Graham and Slee's (2005) criticism that the appealing concept of inclusion is often used as a means of "explaining and protecting the status quo" (p. 3).

For example, the video's upbeat outlook implies that the various forms of social inequality that led to historical practices of exclusion are a thing of the past. Students with learning disabilities and physical disabilities, students from cultural and linguistic minority groups, and homosexual students are all shown as happily participating in the educational and social activities in their school, receiving appropriate support when necessary (peer and teacher support, assistive technology, adaptations to the physical space, a gay-straight alliance club), and enjoying broad acceptance of their peers and teachers. There is no mention of students with emotional and behavioural disabilities (EBD). It might be argued that despite the soundness of the discrete forms of support and accommodation portrayed in the video, supporting any of these groups of learners would, in practice, be a more complicated enterprise than the video suggests. Moreover, the needs of the group of learners that is considered the source of greatest concern to teachers (Alberta Education, 2008; Cook, 2001) – students with severe EBD – did not appear to warrant even the sort of generalized mention received by the other groups.

Again, Alberta Education's move to diversity could be seen as the call to remedy-through-inclusion, which is conveniently, by their accounts, already happening. This allows the current conservative agenda of accountability through standardization to continue (Giroux, 2006) while idealizing inclusion as something well on its way. Like Jahnukainen (2011), we believe that a neo-liberal market ideology via accountability measures (standardized tests), choice (charter and private schools), and publication of test results (for the public and by the government for school boards) are general policies and practices that can block an inclusive education system because school cultures tend to become overly focused on "results" as success rather than social democracy.

Likewise, given that one of the new values for education in Alberta is an "entrepreneurial spirit" (Alberta Education, 2011a), we wonder how much these reforms cater to a conservative political agenda to keep Alberta "economically competitive". What place do "disabled" students have in that agenda, especially given the rapid rise of other world economies? For example, in Alberta Education's *Action Plan for Education* (2011):

> The continued development of a highly-skilled, knowledgeable, innovative and productive workforce is critical to ensuring that Alberta sustains its competitive advantage in a global economy, allowing the province to attract investment, and high value-added industries. Alongside its role in strengthening the economy, the ECS-12 education system will continue to teach the qualities and characteristics of citizenship, which are essential to building communities across Alberta (p. 3).

A similar situation has already played out in New South Wales, Australia (Graham and Jahnukainen, 2011). Inclusive language shifted back to that of integration; changes in the School Act gave schools boards greater powers to remove students with emotional and behavioural challenges, and additional funding is framed as, in the words of Graham and Jahnukainen, "'something extra' for those who cannot meet the standards by way of 'general' provision" (p. 268). In Alberta, this is officially called "accommodation" (Alberta Education, 2006) and is post-hoc to instructional planning for "mainstream" or normal learners.

We are led to ask: How can we call our educational system inclusive, as a place of beliefs and practices that value diversity as human life (Stiker, 1999, p. 8), while at the same time directly frame children and youth who are different as disabled, sick, or abnormal? Slee's (2011) assertion comes to mind: "The story of inclusive education is also the story of the reworking of a concept to render it compatible with the priorities of power. It is a story of the assignation of values; it is the story of those who are and those who are not valued" (p. 191). Feedback from the public during the *Setting the Direction* initiative echoed our concern: "If you say ALL students, you should mean ALL students" (Alberta, 2009, p. 14).

What Happened to Action on Inclusion?

We question whether the inclusion projects are archived because as is indicated on the Alberta Education website, they are indeed 'shelved' projects, or whether the new Minister of Education is attempting to move them forward once again.

In a recent professional development presentation with an Alberta Education Inclusive Education Manager, we were told that while the *Action on Inclusion* project was announced, the results from a larger consultation with the citizens of the province had just started to take shape and suggested that the entire school system needed reformation (Alberta Education, 2012b). This was known as the *Inspiring Action on Education Initiative*, which included discussions with all Albertans about broad-based topics on education including inclusion, curriculum, technology, and parental and community engagement (Alberta, 2010). *Action on Inclusion* was put on hold while these larger reforms were being discussed. One outcome of this and several other initiatives by Alberta Education was an extensively revised School Act, December 10, 2012 (Alberta, 2012d).

Indeed, a province-wide curriculum re-design is afoot, including a re-envisioning of the educational values around core competencies, rather than curriculum objectives (Alberta Education, 2011a). Despite this, Alberta Education believes there is still a need for special education in the province. This is evidenced on its website with the continued posting of disability-specific support documents that continue to address disability singularly through a deficit framing (Alberta Education, 2012a). It is also apparent in the continued reliance on a system of provincial standardized testing that demands students provide "proof of disability" in order to be eligible for testing accommodations (Williamson & Paul, 2012). We believe there may be educational reform on the horizon, but it appears these reforms will continue to sit upon traditional special education and the deficit model of disability.

We are not alone in our concerns. The head of the Alberta Teachers' Association research branch, J-C Couture wrote in 2012:

The Alberta government's policy on inclusion in schools has become reminiscent of ancient palimpsests by continually reoccupying the same space with an unending series of revisions, scribblings and new texts. It's not that the intent is malicious– it's just doing the same thing over and over (p. 54).

As a result of these turns back to the special education tradition, we believe the government and school boards are still talking about inclusion in a way that reflects what Slee (2011) has termed "neo-special education" (p. 63): the co-opting and appropriation of inclusion by traditional special education. In this appropriation, more current special education students are invited into regular classrooms with stronger forms of post-hoc differentiation and accommodation, educators teach under the continued reign of the traditional pathology of students into disabled categories of abnormality, and Alberta's educational system is deemed to be more inclusive.

A Stalled Journey to Inclusion or A Cautious One? Where Are We Now?

Alberta Education's website currently emphasizes a commitment to inclusive education though also notes that change will take time. Some significant changes have occurred this year. The coding criteria booklet (Alberta Education, 2012c), published yearly, no longer requires the severe emotional and behavioural disability codification process to include updated formal assessments from psychologists or psychiatrists after the first initial assessment. In the past, a formal reassessment was required every three years. This requirement, inherent to the bounty system, resulted in school board psychologists spending most of their time on psychological assessments. As early as 2001, Janzen and Carter wrote of the increased pressure on school psychologists to complete paperwork necessary for government funding. Specht (2013) argued that assessments have always been one of the priorities for school psychologists. Unfortunately, as we have shared, that resource-intensive work on behalf of the acquisition of further support for individually coded students did not measure up against

Alberta Education criteria: Most of the severe codes in the province came from the EBD category, and half of those failed the review:

> Special education funding in Alberta would better serve students who are diagnosed with emotional and/or behavioural disabilities if there was a base level of funding provided that was not attached to coding. Schools would not have to engage in extensive, time-consuming coding processes in order to access needed resources. It is highly detrimental to meeting students' needs to have the funding system leading the pedagogical decision-making, labeling students inappropriately and watering down the real meaning of 'severe disability' or 'severe behavioural disturbance', which has (and still is in many other countries/regions) been relatively rare and associated directly with mental illnesses. (Wishart & Jahnukainen, 2010, pp. 185 - 186).

The province seems to now understand that directly assisting all students in schools, rather than employing psychologists to constantly assess particular students for disabilities, is a better use of school resources. For example, in one of Alberta's urban public school boards, school psychologists can now be regularly found working alongside teachers in specialized classrooms. Parrish's (2001) major review of special education spending in the US (used by the *Setting the Direction* policy forming group) found that only about 62% of special education dollars went directly to students (p. 13). As of this year, school boards can use other informal means of re-assessment to help determine the best needs for students, giving them the flexibility to direct resources.

Also for the 2012 school year, the province stopped the funding for severe disabilities and replaced it with an inclusive education funding initiative. This funding model is based on assumptions of what special needs services should be required to provide services for the entire student population. This is known as a census model:

> Advantages associated with such a system are that it is very simple and has very limited administrative requirements. It also tends to

allow a great deal of local flexibility in that it creates no fiscal incentive for putting a student in one placement or category of disability over another. In the case of the census-basis for determining the flat grant amount, it also does not create an incentive for placing students in special education (Parrish, 2001, p. 10).

This additional student money is allocated in block funding while extra funding is provided for differential factors. These factors are based on a formula that uses census data such as the number of single-parent families and household income. However, there are disadvantages to the census model, which is perhaps why Alberta Education also included the differential model of extra inclusive funding. This funding attempts to account for actual regional differences in student populations. Taking into account factors like income levels and single-parent families could also be interpreted as an acknowledgement that disability is more complex than the logic of inherent abnormality: Social capital plays a role in the creation of disabling learning conditions (Thomas, 2012). The census model also runs the risk of coming under threat because dollars are no longer earmarked to particular students (Parrish, 2001).

In the first year of the census model, Alberta school boards received no less than they normally would have under the previous funding model. However, it is important to note that the previous severe disabilities funding was frozen for three years while the *Setting the Direction* and *Action on Inclusion* projects were in review. Some educators claim that the current inclusive education funding model is not really "extra" money, but rather money school boards should have had each year for the past three years.

Regardless, funding is now provided based on a model meant to be used for all students in need – a need determined at the discretion of each school board. A recent landmark Supreme Court decision regarding student rights to the provision of special education supports and services in the province of British Columbia, Canada states that "the onus is on school boards to allocate funding in a way that students with special needs get the supports they require to have meaningful access to education. Doing any less amounts to unlawful discrimination" (Teghtmeyer, 2012). On the one hand, this seems encouraging because it requires school boards to provide appropriate education for all students and, at least at the level of recent institutional rhetoric, the more inclusive education is, the more meaningful it will be. On the other hand, it remains potentially problematic because it may, depending on institutional/legal interpretations of meaningful access to education, actually support the continued segregation of students under the popular learning and medically-influenced beliefs. How this plays out will depend on future interpretations of the Supreme Court ruling.

The stakeholders invited to participate in the consultation process for *Setting the Direction* (Alberta Education, 2009) included parents, advocacy groups for people with disabilities, and private schools that cater to students with disabilities. While many spoke to their hopes for a more inclusive education system, others worried that the proposed reforms would result in the cutting of services for students with disabilities and a blurring of institutional accountability (Alberta Education, 2009). With a very active public shaping educational policy in Alberta, we fear that the normalization of disability as a rights discourse will empower stakeholders who continue to support the segregated model. At the core of the inclusion debate is discussion around the definition of meaningful education for all students. For example, we know that at least some school boards in Alberta still use the disability-codification model as criteria for access to specialized classrooms and supports. We suggest that this sustains a traditional special education system that is parallel to and different from "regular" education, despite the ubiquitous claims of learning for each and every student today.

Though these changes to the funding model may influence more inclusive practices at the school level, we also note that the only substantial province-wide changes resulting from *Action on Inclusion* before it was shelved were the adjustments to policies directly or indirectly (through diagnostic proof of disability) related to funding. While funding has remained constant or increased, and schools boards have been given greater autonomy to use the funds as deemed appropriate to support students, the relative stability of the block/census funding formula has inoculated Alberta Education from the costly vagaries that the rapid increase in severe disability diagnoses/codes would have entailed under the per-severely disabled student funding system. Whether the intent of this economic reform was informed more by the need for greater justice for students or for more manageable forecasting of funding obligations for special education, it does, pragmatically, seem to have the potential to help alleviate the various sicknesses brought forth by the bounty phenomenon.

We continue, however, to await the resumption of the discussion of meaningful change, beyond economic reform, that stalled with the shelving of the *Action on Inclusion* project. As the Alberta Teachers' Association (ATA) President wrote in the spring of 2012, the Education Minister of the time "failed to even mention special education or *Setting the Direction*" in his announcement of the government's newest plan for education in the province (p. 59). Speaking on behalf of the ATA, she also wrote, "we have consulted with our education stakeholders, yet we have heard nothing from government" (p. 59). With the very recent release of an austerity budget the likes of which Alberta has not seen for approximately 15 years, we wonder if the conversation has the space to continue at all.

With its reforms to date, Alberta Education seems to have largely dealt with the bounty phenomenon, albeit with a model that also has the potential to fund more inclusively. Given the pervasiveness of the medicalized model of disability and the policies and programs it has informed, however, considerable concern and effort is still required to support all educators and students in creating more inclusive educational settings.

References

Alberta Education. (2006). Identifying student needs: Selecting accommodations and strategies. Edmonton, AB.

Alberta Education. (2008). Report on Severe Disabilities Profile Review. Edmonton, AB.

Alberta Education (Producer). (2009). Video Message from Minister. Available from http://education.alberta.ca/department/ipr/inclusion/settingthedirection/phasei.aspx

Alberta Education. (2009a). Setting the direction for special education in Alberta: Phase 2 community consultation what we heard report. Calder Bateman Communications for Alberta Education Government of Alberta: Edmonton, AB.

Alberta Education. (2009b). Setting the Direction Framework. Retrieved June 19, 2011 from http://www.education.alberta.ca/media/.../sc_settingthedirection_framework.pdf

Alberta Education. (2010). Inspiring Action on Education. Government of Alberta: Edmonton, AB.

Alberta Education. (2011). Action Plan for Education. Government of Alberta: Edmonton, AB.

Alberta Education. (2011a). Framework for student learning: Competencies for engaged thinkers and ethical citizens with an entrepreneurial spirit. Retrieved from: http://education.alberta.ca/department/ipr/curriculum/framework.aspx

Alberta Education. (2011b). Handbook for the Identification and Review of Students with Severe Disabilities 2011/2012. Retrieved from: http://education.alberta.ca/media/841679/hdbk_severedisabilities.pdf

Alberta Education (Producer). (2012). Diversity in Alberta Schools a Journey to Inclusion. Available from http://ideas.education.alberta.ca/engage/about-engagement/what's-new

Alberta Education. (2012a). Government of Alberta - Education - Initiatives, Projects and Reviews–Inclusive Education. Retrieved from http://www.education.alberta.ca/department/ipr/Inclusion.aspx

Alberta Education. (2012b). Inspiring Action on Education. Retrieved from: http://ideas.education.alberta.ca/engage/

Alberta Education. (2012c). Special Education Coding Criteria 2012/2013. Retrieved from: http://education.alberta.ca/media/825847/spedcodingcriteria.pdf

Alberta Education. (2012d). Education Act 2012. Retrieved from: http://www.education.alberta.ca/department/policy/education-act.aspx

Alberta School Boards Association. (2011). Zone 2/3 general meeting minutes and director's report March 25, 2011. Retrieved from: http://www.asba.ab.ca/files/pdf/zone23_min_mar11.pdf

Alberta Teachers' Association. (2002). A brief history of public education in Alberta: Monograph. Edmonton, AB: Alberta Teachers' Association.

Alberta Teachers' Association. (2012). Inclusive Education: What make us diverse makes us strong. *ATA Magazine*. Edmonton, AB: Alberta Teachers' Association.

Biesta, G., & Burbules, N.C. (2003). *Pragmatism and educational research*. Lanham, MD: Rowman & Littlefield.

Chapman, J. (2003). Tragedy and catastrophe: Contentious discourses of ethics and disability. *Journal of Intellectual Disability Research*, 47, 540-547.

Cook, B. (2001). A comparison of teachers' attitudes toward their included students with mild and severe disabilities. *The Journal of Special Education, 34*(4), 203.

Davey, N. (2006). *Unquiet understanding: Gadamer's philosophical hermeneutics.* Albany: State: University of New York Press.

Dechant, G.M., & Muttart Foundation. (2006). *Winter's children: The emergence of children's mental health services in Alberta,* 1905-2005. Edmonton, AB: Muttart Foundation.

Gabel, S. L., & Danforth, S. (2008). *Disability and the politics of education: An international reader.* New York, NY: Peter Lang.

Gadamer, H.G. (1976). *Philosophical hermeneutics.* Berkeley, CA, USA: University of California Press.

Gadamer, H.G., Dutt, C., & Palmer, R. E. (2001). *Gadamer in conversation: Reflections and commentary.* New Haven: Yale University Press.

Gadamer, H.G. (2004). *Truth and method.* London: Continuum.

Gilham, C.M. (2012). The Privileges Chart in a Behaviour Class: Seeing the Power and Complexity of Dominant Traditions and Unconcealing Trust as Basic to Pedagogical Relationships. *Journal of Applied Hermeneutics.*

Gilham, C.M. (2012). From the Science of Disease to the Understanding of Those Who Suffer: The Cultivation of an Interpretive Understanding of Behaviour Problems in Children. *Journal of Applied Hermeneutics.*

Giroux, S.S. (2006). *Playing in the Dark: Racial Repression and the New Campus Crusade for Diversity.* College Literature, 33(4), 93-112.

Goffman, E. (1963). Stigma: *Notes on the management of spoiled identity.* Englewood Cliffs, NJ: Prentice-Hall.

Graham, L. J., & Jahnukainen, M. (2011). Wherefore art thou, Inclusion? Analysing the development of inclusive education in New South Wales, Alberta and Finland. *Journal of Educational Policy*, 26(2), 263-288.

Graham, L. & Slee, R. (2005, November). Inclusion? Australian Association for Research in Education Annual Conference, Sydney, AUS.

Graham, L., & Slee, R. (2008). An Illusory Interiority: Interrogating the discourse/s of Inclusion. *Educational Philosophy and Theory*, 40(2), 277-293.

Hacking, I. (1998). *Mad travelers: Reflections on the reality of transient mental illnesses*. Charlottesville, VA: University Press of Virginia.

Hacking, I. (2004). *Historical Ontology*. New York, NY: Harvard University Press.

Heidegger, M. (1962). *Being and Time* (J. R. Macquarrie, E., Trans.). New York, NY: Harper Collins.

Husserl, E. (1970). *The crisis of European sciences and transcendental phenomenology: An introduction to phenomenological philosophy*. Evanston: Northwestern University Press.

Illich, I. (1976). *Medical nemesis: The expropriation of health*. New York, NY: Pantheon Books.

Jahnukainen, M. (2011). Different Strategies, Different Outcomes? The History and Trends of the Inclusive and Special Education in Alberta (Canada) and in Finland. Scandinavian *Journal of Educational Research*, 55(5), 489-502. DOI: 10.1080/00313831.2010.537689

Janzen, H.L., & Carter, S. (2001). State of the art of school psychology in Alberta. Canadian *Journal of School Psychology*, 16(2), 79-84.

Jardine, D.W. (2000).*Under the tough old stars: Ecopedagogical essays*. Brandon, MB: The Foundation for Educational Renewal.

Jardine, D.W., Friesen, S., & Clifford, P. (2006). *Curriculum in Abundance.* New Jersey, NY, USA: Lawrence Erlbaum Associates.

Jardine, D.W., Frieson, S., & Clifford, P. (2008). *Back to the Basics of Teaching and Learning: Thinking the World Together.* New York, NY: Routledge.

Kauffman, J. M., Crockett, J. B., Gerber, M. M., & Landrum, T. J. (2007). Achieving *the radical reform of special education: Essays* in honor of James M. Kauffman. New York, NY: Lawrence Erlbaum Associates.

Kearney, R. (2011). What is Diacritical Hermeneutics? *Journal of Applied Hermeneutics.* Taken from: http://jah.synergiesprairies.ca/jah/index.php/jah/article/download/6/7

Nussbaum, M.C. (2006). *Frontiers of justice: Disability, nationality, species membership.* Cambridge, MA: The Belknap Press.

Parrish, T.B. (2001). Special Education in an Era of School Reform: Special Education Finance. Federal Resource Centre. Retrieved from: http://education.alberta.ca/department/ipr/inclusion/settingthedirection/library.aspx

Porter, J.I. (1997). Foreword to D. Mitchell and S. Snyder (Eds). *The Body and Physical Difference.* Ann Arbor, University of Michigan Press. (pp. xii - xiv).

Reindal, S. M. (2009). Disability, capability, and special education: towards a capability-based theory. *European Journal of Special Needs Education*, 24: 2, 155-168.

Ricoeur, P. (2007). *Reflections on the just.* Chicago, IL: University of Chicago Press.

Skrtic, T. (1995). *Disability and democracy: Reconstructing (special) education for post modernity.* New York, NY: Teachers College Press.

Slee, R. and Allan, J. (2001). Excluding the Included: A recognition of inclusive education. *International Studies in Sociology of Education*, 11:2, 173-191.

Slee, R. (2011). *The irregular school: exclusion, schooling, and inclusive education.* New York, NY: Routledge.

Specht, J.A. (2013). Mental Health in Schools: Lessons Learned From Exclusion. *Canadian Journal of School Psychology.*

Stiker, H.J. (1999). *A history of disability.* University of Michigan, Michigan, USA: University of Michigan.

Teghtmeyer, J. (2012). Adequate special education is not a dispensable luxury. *Alberta Teachers' Association News:* Vol. 47, No. 7. Retrieved from http://www.teachers.ab.ca/Publications/ATA%20News/Volume%2047% 202012-13/Number%207/Pages/Adequate-special-education.aspx

Thomas, G. (2012). A review of thinking and research about inclusive education policy, with suggestions for a new kind of inclusive thinking. *British Educational Research Journal:* DOI: 10.1080/01411926.2011.652070

Thomas, G., & Loxley, A. (2007). *Deconstructing special education and constructing inclusion:* Berkshire, England: Open University Press.

Tremain, S. (2005). *Foucault and the government of disability.* University of Michigan, USA: University of Michigan Press.

Valle, J.W., & Connor, D. J. (2011). *Rethinking disability: A disability studies approach to inclusive practices.* New York, NY: McGraw-Hill.

Weinsheimer, J. (1991). *Gadamer's Metaphorical Hermeneutics.* In H. J. Silverman (Ed.), *Gadamer and Hermeneutics,* (pp. 181-201) New York, NY: Routledge.

Williamson, W. J., & Paul, W. J. (2012). The Level Playing Field: Unconcealing Diploma Exam Accommodation Policy. *Journal of Applied Hermeneutics, pages 1 - 16.*

Winzer, M.A. (2009). *From integration to inclusion: A history of special education in the 20th century.* Washington, DC, USA: Gallaudet University Press.

Wishart, D. and M. Jahnukainen (2010). Difficulties associated with the coding and categorization of students with emotional and behavioural disabilities in Alberta. *Emotional and Behavioural Difficulties*, 15(3), 181-187.

Wrathall, M. (2010). *Heidegger and Un-concealment: Truth, Language and History.* New York, NY: Cambridge University Press.

Chapter 4: Perspectives of Inclusion – Sketches of Beginning Possibilities in an Alberta-Finland Partnership

Kathy Olmstead

Assistant Superintendent, Learning Services, Livingstone Range School Division, Alberta

If I say the word "inclusion" aloud in a current educational setting, there will be a reaction. This reaction could be a grimace, it could be a glint in someone's eyes, or it could be a group's somewhat silent groan as in "here we go again." A student could be worried about her visibility in a large class, preferring the safety of a small group of students just like her. A teacher might be visualizing the last time he was publicly called a nasty name by one of his students. Parents could be concerned that their child doesn't have an assigned teacher assistant this year. A school principal might be remembering how a group of seven year olds assisted another child with his feeding tube just as a matter of course. This reaction could be positive or negative or a combination of both. But there will be a reaction. People have to give something up to move forward. The notion of inclusion evokes people's passions. People's perspectives of how inclusion will affect them evoke passions – passions of perspective.

I am immersed in these passions of perspective. In my 30 years as an elementary and secondary classroom teacher, school administrator, and now jurisdictional leader in rural Alberta, I have worked to become immersed. I have worked to hear varied perspectives as we – students, parents, teachers and principals – struggle to assist each and every student find her way to success. I have worked to juggle these perspectives within broader community expectations. I have my own perspective. Be forewarned, I am writing from an admitted passion for a fully inclusive society that welcomes and lives safely side by side with each other – even those we did not choose to live close by; a passion that frowns on our current need to categorize and sort children by their weaknesses in order to plan school programming; a passion for shifting our focus to children's strengths and talents as the basis for their learning. To support this complex conversation and to move toward more inclusive learning environments, I will use the word inclusion as defined by a leading researcher in the field, Mel Ainscow and his colleagues (2008):

> [Inclusion is] a *principled approach to education* [original emphasis], which involves: the process of increasing the participation of students in, and reducing their exclusion from, the curricula, cultures and communities of local schools; restructuring the cultures, policies and practices in schools so that they respond to the diversity of students in their locality; the presence, participation and achievement of all students vulnerable to exclusionary pressures, not only those with impairments or those who are categorized as "having special educational needs" (p. 20).

I am attached to this definition for four main reasons. First, Ainscow works from a *principled* perspective, ever reminding us that our values and beliefs need to act as our filter system in making decisions, and they are not just words to post on the wall. Second, increasing all students' participation is the key message, even in curricula where we most often pathologize students' failures and, in our remediation attempts, exclude them further. Third, I love that Ainscow speaks to *exclusion*, keeping us honest that many of our practices do just that – exclude – and we need to notice any child that is vulnerable to this exclusion for *any* reason. And lastly, we need to respond to students *in their locality*. Local school and community personnel need the permission, the responsibility and the resources to support students and families. Decisions *are* best made closest to the child as we build relationships and understandings with each other. Ainscow's definition of *inclusion* is more *inclusive* in its own right as it insists that as educators, we restructure our work and our work places, instead of asking all children to either fit into our current categories or go elsewhere. This is my work.

Using my passion for this work, I currently have the privilege to participate in a partnership with our Alberta Teachers' Association and the Finnish National Board of Education, a partnership that has and does promote ongoing dialogue amongst students, teachers and principals from both contexts. Working together in larger symposium-type settings and specific school visits over the past two years, I have joined individuals from five specific schools in each country as they define their journey in making "a great school for *all*" (Alberta Teachers' Association, 2012). Given my current work with school principals in Livingstone Range School Division, my focus in this journey is on the role of the school principal. What do these school-based leaders see as important in the design of great schools for all students? What are the challenges they meet – especially given their leadership roles and responsibilities? What *possibilities* do we see in one another's work?

I chose to focus on school principals as I see their work as crucial to juggling the multiple passions of perspective toward inclusion. Principals balance the workings of our classrooms and the world outside the walls of the school. They are close enough to students to enable responsive decision-making, yet the complexities involved can be overwhelming. As a principal's effect on student learning is second only to that of classroom teachers (Leithwood, Harris and Hopkins, 2008), time spent on better understanding their roles and how we design and support these roles will be time well spent in our shift to increasingly inclusive practices.

With this premise in mind, I accompanied two teachers and an administrator from our Crowsnest Consolidated High School to Finland for a total of 10 days in the spring of 2012 to listen to and learn from some of their students, teachers and administrators. In this short time, I participated in discussions with those directly involved in the partnership from both Finland and Alberta and visited comprehensive (Grades 1-9) as well as Upper Secondary and Vocational High Schools representative of both rural and urban areas. I also spent some time in conversation with personnel at the University of Helsinki, Faculty of Education. Everyone opened their doors, welcoming me into their spaces and thoughts. The resulting sketches, drawn with an inclusive education perspective, beg further discussion but offer beginning *possibilities* – possibilities prevalent in the work of both jurisdictions and some specific to Finland. Five different figures are emerging from my first glimpses into the work of these school leaders – outlines of local decision-making, shared school leadership, student governance, assessment practices, and the blending of special and general education. Each comes with its respective challenges but challenges that are worth the effort when seen in the light of their possibilities. I invite you to consider these five sketches as beginning steps in further realizing inclusion.

Possibilities

Local Decision-Making

Both Alberta and Finland decentralize their decision-making to allow school jurisdictions to foster democratic decision-making principles. Broad guidelines for our elected school boards and Finland's elected municipalities give them responsibility and latitude to build and organize school communities that meet local needs. Likewise, schools often organize and govern their own school communities. Although challenges inherent to "deliberative democracy" (Guttman and Thompson, 2004) are not always well defined and the needed ongoing debate with communities is messy, it will increase participation in our conversations and help our communities better understand our goals and methods. Further development of assurance frameworks (Murgatroyd, 2011) that allow and indeed expect schools to report their progress with locally designed artifacts and measures is needed in the Alberta context to meet our accountability requirements and yet better respect the local decision-making context. Picture the possibilities inherent in students, parents, staff, and community all engaged democratically in the design and workings of their schools.

Sharing School Leadership

Shared school-based leadership is evident in both Alberta and Finland although it varies greatly in specific schools and is still textured with hierarchies. The school principal is in charge and s/he distributes leadership as they see fit so structures vary considerably from school to school. In both contexts, the pressures on this individual are immense, and we are working to understand how to organize and better support this role.

Teaming is one such structure of support. Learning Support Teams in Livingstone Range School Division and Student Welfare Groups across Finland are designed to bring needed professionals together to work with parents to support any student who struggles. These teams can include Learning Support or Special Education Teachers, a School Principal, Counsellors, Specialized Literacy and/or Numeracy Teachers and in Finland's case, Public Health Nurses. Alberta is currently working to better include Rehabilitation, Mental Health, and Family Support services in these school teaming processes. If a student's struggles become the regular focus for these professionals from different disciplines *together at one table*, imagine the possibilities for the design of responsive programming.

Tying the thoughts and work of this school-based support team to other teams of educators in the school is necessary for their success. This connection can be a challenge as was evidenced in both contexts – in finding the time to meet together and in engaging staff. Classroom teachers need a space to bring their concerns about a child's learning forward with each other and then with the Learning Support Team. Likewise, Learning Support Team members need time and space to work with classroom teachers, students, and parents. This back and forth conversation is crucial if we are to quickly identify barriers to a student's success and assist their continued participation. Picture the possibilities in such a fluid responsiveness.

Student Governance

Where are students in shared leadership? Students need to be in the foreground of the drawing, especially if we hope to live up to any democratic ideals. Students can take responsibility for their own learning and in caring for each other in the process. Structuring our school environments to allow spaces for them to bring forward what they think and believe, to commit themselves and follow through on actions that contribute, to challenge others when they see unjust practices – ensures those who are most affected have a voice and builds capacities for democratic decision-making.

Schools in both Alberta and Finland allow students the beginnings of voice. Student leadership is most often elected and takes on activities that foster student engagement. Both contexts would benefit from a more deliberate involvement of students in the day-to-day and longer-term governance of schooling. Students in kindergarten are more than able to say what they think if asked, and by high school age students can be expected to participate as adults – *if* they see their viewpoint as useful and *if* they understand how to contribute. The deliberate involvement of students contributes two-fold – by bringing more ideas and possibilities to the table and by fostering an involvement that will follow them into other communities. This shift is a difficult shift to make – a shift from adult-led, often compliance-based learning environments to schools that design space for each and every student to come forward with their ideas and *effect decision-making*. The rules will need to change. But picture the possibilities!

Assessment Practices

Expectations for teacher practice in both Alberta and Finland are high, and as students in both systems are successful on international benchmarks, clearly our teachers live up to those expectations. Finland has an advantage in the area of classroom assessment practices that we need to heed. Teachers in Finland shoulder the responsibility and are trusted to assess and report on a student's learning – to the student, to the parents, to the local school community and in a generalized way to the larger community. Externally designed system-wide assessments are only used once students are finished school to assist in supporting post-secondary decisions. In elementary and secondary schools, classroom teachers are supported and trusted to understand students, plan needed programming and report their progress. Therefore they feel competent in doing so.

Alberta's educational community relies on external assessments from 'experts' and has done so through much of its history, from both a systems perspective in the use of standardized achievement examinations and a classroom basis in the use of purchased normed tools or contracted 'specialists'. Consequently, teachers often do not have the confidence in themselves to utilize the varied, rich data they collect on a daily basis to communicate a student's learning strengths and needs. In Alberta, we continue to ask for outside experts to come in and paint the picture for teachers to work with. No wonder they sometimes want someone else to 'fix' a student. We need to use teachers' assessment results to inform students, parents, communities and the province of our students' successes and needs and then plan accordingly: In doing so we will professionalize the profession. Assessment and reporting practices must move from the classroom out to the systems – not the other way around. This challenge requires a huge mind shift from our current practices of accountability *to those outside* the system to practices that are responsible first to students, but is worth it if we are truly to foster trust in our democratic practices. Picture the possibilities inherent in preparing, supporting, and trusting our teachers.

Blending General and Special Education Services

We must discontinue the practice of separating our students who do not fit the current norm. As our diversity increases, so do the numbers of categories and slots. Upon examination of these slots in Alberta, it is obvious that a disproportionate number of First Nations students, students from lower socio-economic levels, students new to our country, and especially students who would fit in more than one of these groups, are now 'coded' and receiving in most cases, separate, exclusive 'supports'.

These needed supports have created a bureaucratic realm: Each code comes with its own set of programs, classrooms, and in some cases, its own schools. To complicate factors, large-scale provincial student assessments have grown hand in hand with the special education focus, and schools need their students to do well on these external measures. Required curricula are dense with as many as 1,200 outcomes for one student in a school year. Teachers, relying on the special education department, learn to send a student out for special assessments and placement as soon as they see a student isn't learning, as they *should be*. Through the individual pathologizing of a student's learning struggle (Liaisidou, 2011, p. 891) we put the onus squarely on the student if they fail. There is something wrong with her. First Nations families are especially fearful of this system as it hearkens back to residential school settings in colonial Canada, where mental illness was used as a reason to lock someone away, especially when noncompliant. Even as we profess to believe in and move to more inclusive educational environments, the system sustains itself with its categorizations.

We can learn a lot from Finland in this area. They have an inclusive system to assist students with what we would call mild or moderate learning concerns. As discussed above, their Student Welfare Groups meet regularly and support teachers with all students as their needs arise. These supports include co-teaching, working with small groups, individualized assessment or tutoring, and coordination with medical personnel as needed. Students value and search out the supports even in high school. Finland's curricula are designed with broad, open goals that again, trust teachers to assist students with different access points. One Finnish school principal spoke of the design and use of positive discrimination funds – resources allocated to focus on any student needing extra supports; resources entrusted to schools to use for these extra supports; resources allocated without a lot of added 'red tape'. Finland has the policy and structures in place to potentially support their increasing diversity *and* the increased inclusion of students with more pronounced needs.

Alberta Education's (2012) recent draft of "Planning for a Continuum of Specialized Supports and Services," the redesign of regional collaborative services and our non-enveloped Inclusive Education Funding all have the *potential* to assist with these changes in Alberta. Our challenges will be to realize these policy changes and assist school leaders to design the fluidity necessary in one system that recognizes students' strengths and works to meet their needs. We require school policies and practices that do not put up unintentional barriers. Picture the possibilities in policies that pencil in more of our drawing, depicting what we do and *what we want to do* in our inclusive schools.

What's Next?

With these few sketches, the picture is far from complete. It creates more of a series – one that is unfinished with spaces for the growth of these five renderings and the drawing of others. I purposely titled this conclusion "what's next?" as questions enable me to dig deeper to the heart of what is possible and keep me honest and transparent as I formulate answers and/or further questions. How do we, as educators, recognize students vulnerable to exclusion? What part does each school and community member, including students, play in this recognition? How do we support *and not thwart* school-based leadership as they restructure policies and thus practices? How do we support teachers to further 'professionalize'? Do we address the trust concerns openly in Alberta and if so how? Where do we create the spaces to ensure the conversation takes place with all partners? How do we open our minds and hearts to possibilities instead of picturing the 'ideal' successful student? Our drawings have spaces – spaces for contrast and difference as well as commonalities; spaces for the fuzzy messiness of beginnings and the clarity of established practices; negative or empty spaces for thoughts yet to be; spaces for possibilities.

As relationships and trust grow, continued conversation in the Alberta-Finland partnership promises a deeper commitment to looking for such possibilities – bringing perspectives that are not embedded in our own institutional memory and therefore may see barriers or gaps that we alone cannot; perspectives that model different strengths we can emulate; perspectives that allow us to build patterns for working together globally, which we can then extend to include others. We can intentionally move toward the discomforts that arise in encountering difference, recognizing our place of privilege, and become more aware of how to move ethically forward. Picture these possibilities!

References

Ainscow, M. & Miles, S. (2008). Making education for all inclusive: Where next? *Prospects*. 38, 15–34. DOI: 10.1007/s11125-008-9055-0

Alberta Education. (2012). *Planning for a continuum of specialized supports and services*. Edmonton, AB: Alberta Education (Draft document).

Alberta Teachers' Association. (2012). *A Great School for All - Transforming Education in Alberta*. Edmonton, AB. Retrieved from http://www.teachers.ab.ca/SiteCollectionDocuments/ATA/Publications/Research-Updates

Guttman, A. & Thompson, D. (2004). *Why Deliberative Democracy?* NJ: Princeton University Press.

Leithwood, K., Harris, A. & Hopkins, D. (2008). Seven strong claims about successful school leadership, *School Leadership and Management*, 28(1), 27-42.

Liasidou, A. (2011). Unequal power relations and inclusive education policy making: A discursive analytic approach, *Education Policy*, 25(6), 887-907.

Murgatroyd, S. (2011). *Rethinking Education: Learning and the New Renaissance*. Edmonton, AB: *future*THINK Press.

Chapter 5: Two Models of 'Education for All'– A Comparative View on the Inclusive and Special Education Policies in Alberta and Finland

Markku Jahnukainen, PhD

Professor of Special Education, University of Helsinki, Finland

Introduction

Different actors like the European Union, OECD, United Nations and World Bank publish several reports every year related to the quality of living in different countries around the world. The results tend to raise strong emotions, and often it seems that those countries who have succeeded are happy with the measures used while others try to deny their significance (Kangas, 2008), while others explain the results away as best as possible.

There has been a rising interest also on comparative education and creating the global education standards during the last decade (Samoff, 2007, p. 60). The international school attainment tests, many of them administered by the OECD, have offered an interesting platform for comparing the results in different counties. The OECD Pisa surveys (OECD 2000, 2003 and 2006) assessing the mathematical, reading and science skills of 15-year old students may be the most globally known. For some countries, the results have been relatively shocking, and for some countries these international comparisons have been a success story. Many governments all over the world have turned their eyes to the top-performing countries to find explanations for their success.

One of the biggest high-flyers has been Finland. Educational researchers have given credit, for example, to high teacher quality, flexible curriculum and flexible accountability policy (Aho et al., 2006; Välijarvi et al., 2002). However, it is clear that there can also be broader societal factors affecting the educational climate, like an overall commitment to equality and the incorporation of various welfare services (Grubb et al. 2005) and the strong culture of trust (Aho et al. 2006).

This investigation is motivated by the fact that often the Finnish special education system has been mentioned as one of the key factors behind the high performance in international comparisons (e.g. Kivirauma & Ruoho, 2007; Itkonen & Jahnukainen, 2007; Sahlberg, 2007; Moberg & Savolainen, 2007; Simola 2005). This is a highly interesting finding because, until very recently, special education is rarely seen as a contentious area of public policy; instead it has generally seen as a charitable, humanitarian concern (Armstrong, 2005, 135).

About the Challenges of Comparative Research in Special Education

There is a substantial body of research comparing the education systems in different countries. OECD has published different statistics and manuals related also to the special education population (OECD, 2004). However, there are only a few systematically comparative presentations of special education in different countries. For example, McLaughlin et al. (2006) compared the classification systems of children with disabilities in the United States and in the United Kingdom. Itkonen and Jahnukainen (2007, 2010) compared the special education and disability policies in the United States and in Finland. Powell (2011) looked at Germany and the United States. However, the majority of the international comparative research in special education explains the educational situation of students with disabilities in one country, only making the occasional comparison to other countries (see Mazurek & Winzer, 1994; Mitchell, 2005).

The starting point for this study has been the author's scientific interest in international special education. During the years it has become more and more clear that it is a highly challenging task to try to compare the special education systems in different countries. The ready-made information (like public statistics) is often meant for national purposes only, and uncritical use of that information in comparative study is easily biased. The researchers must also have some kind of tacit knowledge of the system to explain the rationale behind the local practices. One technical example of this is that we needed to merge Finnish data from compulsory schools (grades K - 9/optional 10) to data from Finnish upper-secondary schools and secondary vocational institutions to get comparable K-12 information.

At a more general level, the first challenge of comparative work is related to the different organization and ideologies of compulsory schooling. Some countries, like the US and the UK, have a tradition of having a strong private-school sector and only some portion of an age group will enroll in the public schools. And in some countries, like Finland and Sweden, public education has been the major educational route[1]. How should this discrepancy be taken into account when talking about the special education students and inclusion? In this study, I try to also take into account this perspective when defining the state of 'education for all' in our countries under investigation.

Another challenge is that different countries use the same educational concept differently and/or they may have a totally different vocabulary in use. It is well known and often argued that, for example, 'inclusion' is a complex and misused concept (see Mitchell, 2005). There is some kind of common understanding about the meaning of inclusion in theory; however, at a more practical and operational level, we have multiple realities. Also, more specific concepts related to special education needs and placements are used differently. For example, there is a wide variety in labels referring to a disability formerly known as 'mental retardation' (Table 2). It would be an extremely interesting task to investigate which kinds of consequences that different traditions' use of language may have. However, that is beyond the scope of this study.

---

[1] However, there has been a rapid increase of independent schools in Sweden recently (Lundahl, 2012).

Country	
Finland	Delayed development (mild, moderate, severe)
US	Mental retardation / Developmental delay
Canada (Alberta)	Cognitive disability (mild, moderate, severe)
Australia (New South Wales)	Intellectual impairment (mild, moderate, severe)
UK	Learning disability

Table 2: Concepts in use referring to the DSM-IV 'mental retardation' in special education in different countries.

For making meaningful comparisons, the objective has been to gather commensurable information of the current state and historical trend of special needs education from these two regions (Alberta, Canada and Finland, European Union). Educational systems in both locations have actively developed special education services in order to pursue a policy of inclusion over the last decades. The success of Finland on international school achievement tests is well-known, but also Canada has been among the top performers. What makes the comparison between Finland and

Alberta even more significant is that, according to general provincial results from Canada, Alberta is consistently very close to Finland and above the average Canadian achievement (Table 3).

	Canada	Alberta	Finland
2000			
Mathematics	5	3	4
Reading	2	1	1
Science	5	2	3
2003			
Mathematics	5	2	2
Reading	3	1	1
Science	8	3	1

2006			
Mathematics	5	5	1
Reading	4	4	2
Science	2	2	1

Table 3: Ranks of Canada, Finland and the province of Alberta in PISA 2000, 2003 and 2006 (sources: OECD[2] ; Statistics Canada 2007[3]).

This article will offer a snapshot of the educational polices in these regions using existing statistics related to the K-12 schooling, funding and special education arrangements. The findings summarized here are based on a research project funded by the Social Sciences and Humanities Research Council of Canada (SSHRC). The goal of that study was to investigate how the Finnish models differ from some other school systems with developed inclusive and special education systems (Alberta and New South Wales, Australia). Some of the findings summarized here have been previously published with more details elsewhere (e.g. Graham & Jahnukainen, 2011; Itkonen & Jahnukainen, 2010; Jahnukainen, 2011; Wishart & Jahnukainen, 2010).

This paper will consist of case studies (country overviews) and a more detailed analysis of some key factors related to the education system and organizing special education. The data behind this analysis are presented in Table 2 (basic information about student population and special education)

[2] PISA database accessed at http://www.oecd.org/pisa/pisaproducts/

[3] The Performance of Canada's Youth in Science, Reading and Mathematics: 2006 First Results for Canadians Aged 15 accessed at: http://www5.statcan.gc.ca/bsolc/olc-cel/olc-cel?catno=81-590-XIE2007001&lang=eng

and Table 3 (basic information related to population, economy and schooling).

Country Overviews

Alberta Education System
The responsibility for education in Canada rests almost entirely with provincial legislation. Each of the 10 provinces and three territories has its own school system based upon provincial or territorial education legislation that springs from diverse sources. For funding, the western provinces provide a basic instruction block (or core grant) supplemented with specific (categorical) funding for special education pupils (Winzer, 2008).

In Canada, private schools are not as popular as they are in the US or the UK. Even though Alberta is more in favour of private schooling than other provinces, most of the K-12 school students go to public schools (Table 4); however, the private sector is stronger than before. Other than public schools in Alberta, there are private, provincial and federal schools. During the school year, 2006-2007, 41,124 students were enrolled in these non-public schools, and the not-public sector had 6.8 % of the student population (Alberta's total student population was 601,687).

The local education ministry (Alberta Education) introduced its accountability policies (Accountability Framework) more than 10 years ago during a time of restructuring, downsizing and funding cutbacks, and has recently announced that it will replace current Provincial Achievement Tests with new assessments at the beginning of key stages of learning. Alberta Education has tested all children in the core subjects in Grade 3, 6, and 9 in the name of ensuring that the Alberta Education system maintains a high standard.

Special Education
The segregated special education (special schools and special classes) was strong in Canada until the late 1980s (Lupart, 2000). Currently, the official policy of Alberta Education is that students with special needs will be educated in inclusive settings as their first placement option (Alberta

Education, 2004); however, there are no updated statistics about the special education placement (see Table 4), so, basically, we cannot verify the number of students in different special education environments. However, Alberta Education gathers information by the special education category for funding purposes (Figure 8).

Alberta Education (2004) Standards for special education state:

> In Alberta, educating students with special education needs in inclusive settings is the first placement option to be considered by school boards in consultation with parents and, when appropriate, students. Inclusion, by definition, refers not merely to setting but to specially designed instruction and support for students with special education needs in regular classrooms and neighbourhood schools (p. 1).

Individual Program Plans (IPP = IEP) are developed, implemented, and evaluated for each student that is identified as an exceptional learner. For school-aged children, there are 18 categories for exceptional learners (17disabilities and categories of gifted and talented) in use. The basic structure resembles closely the category used at the federal level in the United States and is called a 'disability model' (Itkonen & Jahnukainen, 2010).

Teachers are responsible for developing IPPs and documenting student progress towards learning objectives. Principals are responsible for ensuring the identification of special-needs students and the delivery of special education programming. Each school has a learning team, which provides consultation, planning, and problem-solving related to special needs programming. In 2006-2007, 80,438 students from kindergarten to grade 12 were identified as having an exceptionality. The total number of identified students has continued to grow. The strongest increase has focused on the category of severe physical or medical disability, and at the same time the use of learning disability (LD) has decreased (see Figure 8). This might be linked to the increase of diagnosed ADHD, which is a condition served under the severe physical or medical disability (see also Jahnukainen, 2010;

Wishart & Jahnukainen, 2010). However, it is also possible that the funding mechanism is affecting the use of severe categories instead of non-severe ones.

	Finland	Alberta
Total Enrolment		
1999	879,958	549,064
2006	953,050	560,563
% Change	+8.3%	+2.1%
Number of Special Education (SE) Students (Tier 3)		
1999	31,353	NA
2006	59,615	80,438
% Change	+90.1%	NA
Proportion of SE Students		
1999	3.6%	NA
2006	6.3%	13.4%
Proportion of Students in Special Schools		
1999	1.6%	NA
2006	1.1%	NA
Emotional & Behavioural Disability (EBD)		
1999	3,886	NA
2005	5,631	14,171
% Change	+44.9%	NA
EBD % of Total Enrolment		
1997	0.4%	NA
2005	0.6%	2.6%
Intellectual Disability (ID)		
1999	16,630	NA
2005	22,372	14,708
% Change	+5.3%	NA
ID as % of Total Enrolment		
1999	1.9%	NA
2005	2.3%	2.6%
% Students Born in a Country Other than Test Country	2.5%	10.7% *(Canada Only)*

Table 4: Basic information on the student population in Alberta and in Finland (K-12).

Special Education Funding

In Alberta, students are identified as having special education needs if they meet the criteria for special education "codes" that were developed by the provincial government's department of education (Alberta Education). For school-aged children, there are 18 codes that reflect a wide variety of disabling conditions, ranging from sensory and speech-language impairments, to learning and intellectual disabilities, as well as emotional and behavioural difficulties. There are also codes for students with physical and medical disabilities that impede their learning, as well as a code for intellectual giftedness. While some of the codes conform closely to accepted psychological or medical diagnostic criteria for clinical disorders (e.g. learning disabilities, mental retardation), a formal diagnosis is not required for all codes. Specialized assessments (e.g. psycho-educational) are nevertheless conducted for most students, in order to acquire information about student needs and functioning levels, both for identification purposes and IPP development.

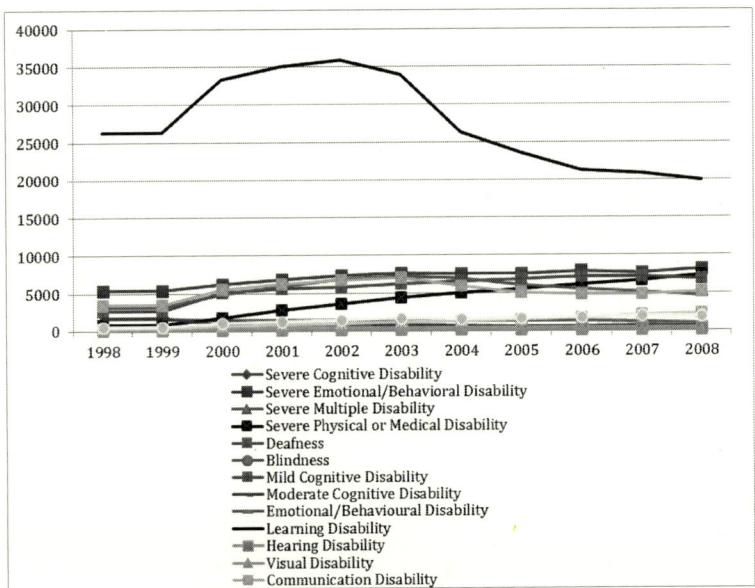

Figure 8: The number of students by the special education category in Alberta 1998 – 2008 (Grades 1 to 12). (Alberta Education, 2009).

The Alberta government classifies the 18 diverse codes into two major categories, that of "severe" disabilities and "mild to moderate" disabilities. However, seven codes fall in the category of severe disabilities. These severe codes represent students with severe to profound retardation (Severe Cognitive Disability); students with clinical disorders that require constant supervision to ensure safety needs (Severe Emotional/Behavioural Disability); students with severe neurological or physical disabilities that require extensive learning modifications and/or personal assistance (Severe Physical or Medical Disability); students with severe vision impairment (Blindness); students with a severe to profound hearing loss (Deafness); students with a severe delay involving language (for kindergarten students only, Severe delay involving language); and students with a combination of two or more moderate-to-severe disabling conditions that are not related (Severe Multiple Disability). The mild to moderate codes thus include students with mild to moderate retardation, learning disabilities, and emotional/behavioural disabilities that do not pose a safety risk to self or others.

The funding mechanism is a combined block funding and 'bounty' strategy (Greene & Forster, 2002). In 2007, Alberta Education provided school boards with $15,751 of special education funding for each student within their jurisdiction that met the eligibility criteria for any of the four severe codes. The remaining 13 mild to moderate codes were supported through the "base instructional funding" that Alberta Education provided to school boards. The amount of base instructional funding that each school board receives is determined on the following basis: school boards currently receive $5,450 for each student in grades one to nine that is enrolled within their jurisdiction. They also receive $155.71 per course credit that each high school student within their jurisdiction completes. These dollar amounts are provided to school boards irrespective of whether students have special educational needs. Although Alberta Education does not specify how much of a school board's base instructional funding should be used on special education, it is expected that school boards draw from this general pool of funding to meet the needs of their students with mild to moderate codes. In other words, unlike the case of severe disabilities, there is no discrete dollar amount that school boards receive for each student who has been identified as having mild to moderate needs.

Finland

Education System
The Finnish education system is based on the idea of 'education for all' since the first Compulsory Education Act 1921 (Jahnukainen, 2003, 2011, 2013). However, it took decades to change the system to be really comprehensive after the tradition of parallel school systems and at least partial exclusion of students with severe disabilities. Finally, since 1997, every school- age child with or without disabilities has been educated in the same comprehensive school system. In practice, this means that almost every child is supposed to enroll in their neighbourhood school. Even though there still exist special schools, the number of special schools and special school placements has been decreasing (Table 4 and Figure 8.). During the compulsory schooling (Grades 1-9), the drop-out rate is very low, around 0.07 %. Some students continue to have an optional extra grade (10) of compulsory schooling before entering into secondary education, which has two main routes: the academic upper-secondary school or the vocational school. Fulltime special education is available only in vocational schools. In Finland, the private sector is very thin; almost every child goes to the neighbourhood school (Table 4). There is no external high-stakes assessment until Year 12. Then the students at the upper-secondary school will participate in the matriculation examination, whose results are partly used as criteria for deciding who sets higher education. The students in the vocational route do not participate in this exam.

Special Education
Until the late 1960s, special education was predominately based in a system of separate special schools and self-contained special classes. The 1970s started the launching of part-time remedial special education, which has since been the expansion of the special education during the 1980s, the main service in special education. Starting from the 1990s, the amount of special schools decreased and, at the same time, the number of students

integrated fulltime in mainstream classes has slowly increased year by year (Figure 9). Even though the inclusion ideology is at least the spirit of the Compulsory Education Act 1998 (came into force 1999) and has been more strongly defined in the recent Amendments to Basic Education Act (2010), the practice of special education is still predominantly integrative and based on the idea of the least restrictive environment.

Finland: Basic Education Act 1998 states:

> If, owing to a disability, an illness, retarded development, an emotional disturbance or a comparable cause, a pupil cannot be otherwise taught, the pupil must be admitted or transferred to special-needs education. As far as possible, special-needs education shall be organised in conjunction with other education or else in a special-needs classroom or some other appropriate facility.

The abovementioned system, with two main service options, has recently been modified to a three-tiered system defined under the title of Learning and Schooling Support (The Amendment of the Basic Education Act 642/2010). Tier 1 (general support) consists of every action made by the regular classroom teacher in terms of differentiation as well as in terms of school-wide efforts to meet the diversity of students. This is basically transferring more responsibility to a classroom teacher as well as the school community. Tier 2 (intensified support) consists of remedial support by the classroom teacher, co-teaching with the special educator and temporal individual or small group learning with the part-time special educator. In practice, this is almost equivalent to the former definition of 'part-time special education'. Tier 3 (special support) consists of the whole continuum of special education services from fulltime general education to a special school placement and is mostly equivalent to the previous 'full time special education'. Every student served at Tier 3 must have an Individualized Education Plan (= IPP).

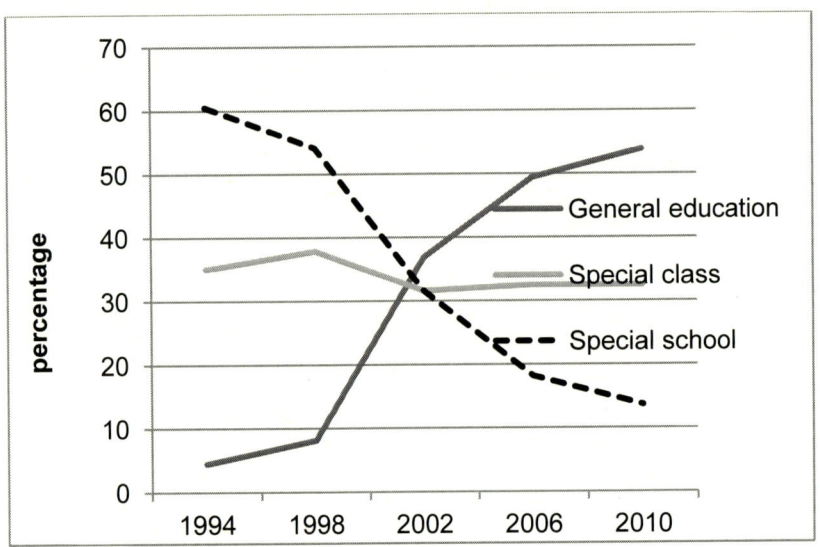

Figure 9: Trends in enrolment of students placed in fulltime special education (Tier 3) in Finland by the placement options[4] calculated as a percentage of total enrolment in Tier 3 level special education in compulsory schools (K – 9/optional 10).

---

[4] General education placement, called 'individual integration'; means that a student with significant special needs is served in a regular classroom full or part-time with IEP and often with the help of a teaching aide. Some of the learning goals may be adjusted in IEP, but not necessarily. If a student with a severe disability is integrated, the maximum size of the teaching group is 20.

Special class means a small teaching group located in mainstream school. The teacher should have special teacher education, and the maximum size of the teaching group is 10. These students may have some integration with regular-class students (e.g. in physical education or based on individual strengths), but the basic placement is in a small group. The learning goals are often somehow adjusted, but individual basis is defined in IEP. Typical groups placed in special classes are students with emotional and behavioural problems, students with neurological disabilities (ADHD, CP syndrome) and students with impaired linguistic development. These groups are considered as benefiting from the smaller size of the group and the help of a specialized teacher.

Special schools are administratively separate special schools which may, however, be located in conjunction with a mainstream school sharing also parts of the school buildings. These schools are mostly specialized in education of some specific disability group, for example, visual impairment, hearing impairment or severe intellectual disabilities. For example, the case of the traditional "deaf schools" is interesting, because the deaf education and Finnish

The very special feature of the Finnish special support system is the extensive use of Tier 2-level part-time special education. The key player in this low-threshold system of meeting the diverse population is a specialized teacher, whose work load is not dedicated to a small group of students only. Instead, s/he is dealing with the whole school population doing assessment, co-teaching, teaching small groups and consulting the classroom teachers (e.g. Rytivaara, Pulkkinen & Takala, 2012). Basically, there is at least one this kind of teacher available in every school. During the school year 2010 – 2011 about 120,000 (or 21.7 percent) comprehensive school students (age group 6 to 16) were using this service. This service holds at the same time a preventive as well as a rehabilitative function. The effectiveness of the Finnish Tier 2 service is based on the premise of early intervention without 'waiting to fail'. In practice, this means that as soon as the classroom teacher or the parents notice that some additional support is needed, the possible intervention can be started. This form of special education is basically open for any students who struggle with learning for whatever reason. There is an intense pressure to rehabilitate the early reading, writing and arithmetic problems using part-time special education.

Funding

The Finnish special education funding was based on the idea that the funding follows the child (referred to as 'bounty' funding by Greene & Forster, 2002) until 2010. Students in need of full-time special education (Tier 3) used to get 1.5-folded funding and a relatively small proportion of students with severe disabilities used to get 2.5-funding compared to other compulsory school students. After 2010, there has not been any extra funding for special education students, except for a small number of students with the most severe disabilities, who will be funded on an individual basis. In general, the state funding for comprehensive schooling is delivered using the estimate calculated based on the census information and the information from the previous school years.

---

sign language are part of the deaf culture; the deaf society is not willing to integrate the students to mainstream schools.

Category	Finland	Alberta
Total Population	5.3 million	3.5 million
GDP[5]	$162 billion	$288 billion
GDP per Capita	$30,734	$80,285
Annual Education Budget (Total)	$9.3 billion	$9.7 billion
K-12 Budget as % of GDP	3.4%	2.4%
K-12 Funding per Capita (Population)	$1,041	$1,968
Number of Students Enrolled K-12	953,050	560,563
Funding per Student K-12 Public and Catholic Schools	$5,787	$12,063
State funding for Students Enrolled in Non-Public Schools	$11.5 million	$140.4 million

---

[5] All currency references converted to US dollars using the purchase power parity (PPP) estimate (OECD, 2009).

Number of Students Enrolled in Non-Public Schools	20,000 (app.)	41,124
Year 12 Retention Rate	89.6%	70.4%

Table 5: Basic information related to population, economy and schooling in Alberta and Finland (school year 2006 -07).

Concluding Comparison: What Makes the Difference?

Based on the basic information gathered for this research, it is clear that there are several major differences between Alberta, Canada and Finland. The homogenous society and lack of ethnic minorities has often been mentioned as one explanation for the recent success of Finland (Sahlberg, 2007). Canada, as well as the United States and Australia, are settlers' societies with a relatively high number of foreign-born residents. Finland is still a relatively homogeneous country, though the migration trends since the early 1990s indicate that Finland is rapidly transforming into a multi-cultural society (Sahlberg, 2007). However, based on the PISA 2006 results, it is clear that Canada, as well as Australia, has been very effective in educating immigrant kids (Figure 10). In countries like Sweden and Finland, the gap between the native and immigrant children is much larger.

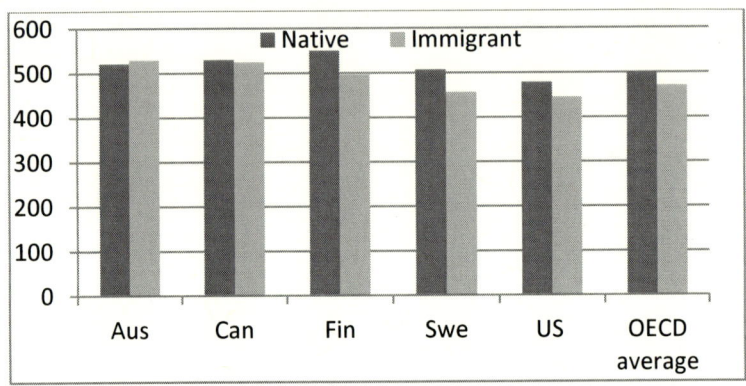

Figure 10: Mean results in PISA 2006 mathematics test by country and the students' origin (Source: OECD [6]).

Though the funding per student in Finland is lower than in Alberta, the higher percentage of the GPD reflects the relative importance of public education in Finnish society. When compared to the extremely neoliberal thinking of New South Wales (Graham & Jahnukainen, 2011), the Alberta model lies somewhere in between with a strong public school system but also an established private sector in education, which is quite small, but the relatively high funding tells us that it is at least moderately valued in Alberta's education policy.

When it comes to organizing the special needs education, it is clear that as long as we are talking about the full-time special education for students with disabilities (Tier 3), the main trends have followed the same kinds of paths. Though the special education system itself, for those who are eligible for full-time special support, is quite the same, there are distinctive differences in actions outside this 'official' special education students' group (i.e. students with disabilities). The Finnish policy underlines the difficulty rather than disability model (Itkonen & Jahnukainen, 2010) and the special educational support is based on observed educational needs rather than rights based on psycho-medical assessment. The main vehicle in this work is the Tier 2 level part-time special education.

---

6 PISA database accessed at http://www.oecd.org/pisa/pisaproducts/

In the current Alberta model, the special education services are mainly based on coded disability categories, and any services outside of that are rare. Even though there is a strong ideological commitment to inclusive education, the system of special needs support eligibility is based on a discrepancy model, and many children must 'wait to fail' before they obtain the services they need. We can speculate that the two-times higher proportion of a Tier 3 level special education student in Alberta, as well as a higher proportion of students with emotional and behavioural disabilities (Table 5), is linked to the omission of low-threshold services available for any students without a heavy assessment procedure.

In general, the Finnish model of 'education for all' is targeting the lowest achieving students and trying to improve the overall standard from there. In other words, the main strategy is to maintain equity and quality education in every school through the comprehensive public school system. The outcomes of this model could be seen also in a lower drop-out rate at the secondary level (Table 5).

In Alberta, partly based on the diverse history, the mixed model of 'education for all' with strong public school, with also support for private, has developed. With this policy, Alberta has really been trying – and also succeeded – in creating a really competitive school system. Having gifted and talented as one category under the exceptionalities/special education is one distinctive feature and tells us about the values regarding the high-achievement as well as the freedom of choice. It could be said that Alberta is trying to offer something for everybody and balance between different cultural and political influences.

Based on this research, as well as in some other comparative approaches (Powell, 2011; Richardson & Powell, 2011), a fair comparison between different school systems in a different context is almost impossible to perform. It is clear that the different socio-political climates have strongly affected the developmental paths of any school system. When it comes to the organizing of the education of students with other than average needs, the political will is regulating the limits of the actions. The comparative research may increase our knowledge of the outcomes of different strategies in a given context, and we might get valuable ideas for improving our own school system. However, any direct policy borrowing or lending should be carefully scrutinized.

References

Act on the Amendment of the Basic Education Act 642/2010 (2010). Helsinki: Government Printing Office.

Aho, E., Pitkänen, K. & Sahlberg, P. 2006. *Policy Development and Reform Principles of Basic and Secondary Education in Finland since 1968*. Washington, DC: World Bank.

Alberta Education. (2004). Standards for Special Education. Retrieved December 2, 2009, from http://education.alberta.ca/department/policy/standards/sestandards.aspx

Alberta Education. (2008a). Annual report 2007-2008. Edmonton, AB: Alberta Education.

Alberta Education. (2008b). Report on severe disabilities profile review. May 2008. Edmonton, AB: Alberta Education.

Alberta Education. (2009). 1997/1998 - 2007/2008 Count of Students Registered in Special Education in Alberta. Unpublished data prepared by Information Services Branch May 1, 2009.

Armstrong, D. (2005). Reinventing inclusion. New labour and the cultural politics of special education. *Oxford Review of Education*, 31 (1), 135–151.

Graham. L.J. & Jahnukainen, M. (2011). Wherefore art thou, inclusion? Analysing the development of inclusive education in New South Wales, Alberta and Finland. *Journal of Education Policy*, 26, 261 – 286.

Greene, J.P. & Forster, G. (2002). Effects of funding incentives on special education enrolment. Civic report 32. New York, NY: Manhattan Institute.

Grubb, N., Jahr, H.M., Neumüller, J. & Field, S. (2005). Finland Country Note for Equity in Education Thematic Review, OECD, http://www.oecd.org/edu/equity/equityineducation

Itkonen, T. & Jahnukainen, M. (2007). An Analysis of Accountability Policies in Finland and the United States. *International Journal of Disability, Development and Education*, 54, 5-23.

Itkonen, T. & Jahnukainen, M. (2010). Disability or Learning Difficulty? Politicians or Educators? Constructing Special Education in Finland and the United States. *Comparative Sociology*, 25, 182 - 201.

Jahnukainen, M. (2003). *The Development of the Education for All in Finland*. In L.H. Hui & R.C. Dowson & M. G. Moont (Eds.) *Inclusive Education in the New Millennium*. Hong Kong: *Education Convergence & The Association for Childhood Education International-Hong Kong & Macau*, 31–38.

Jahnukainen, M. (2010). *Different Children in Different Countries: ADHD in Canada and Finland*. In Graham, L. (Ed.) *(De)Constructing ADHD. Critical Guidance for Teachers and Teacher Education*. Peter Lang, New York, 63–76.

Jahnukainen, M. (2011). Different strategies, different outcomes? The history and trends of the inclusive and special education in Alberta (Canada) and in Finland. *Scandinavian Journal of Educational Research*, 55, 489-502.

Jahnukainen, M. (2013). *Special education in Finland*. In C.R. Reynolds, K.J. Vannest, & E. Fletcher-Janzen (Eds.), Encyclopaedia of special education: A reference for the education of children, adolescents, and adults with disabilities and other exceptional individuals (4th ed.). Hoboken, NJ: John Wiley and Sons, *in press*.

Kangas, O. (2008). Pohjoismaat – mailman paras kolkka? (Nordic countries – the best corner in the world?). *Yhteiskuntapolitiikka*, 73 (4), 357–367.

Kivirauma, J., & Ruoho, K. (2007) Excellence through special education? Lessons from the Finnish school reform. Review of Education, 58, 283–302.

Lundahl, L. (2012). A business like any other? The Swedish upper secondary education market in the early 2000s. In Kivirauma, J., Jauhiainen, A., Seppänen, P. & Kaunisto, T. (Eds). Social perspectives on Education. Research in Educational Sciences 59. Jyväskylä: FERA.

Lupart, J. (2000, April). Students with exceptional learning needs: At-risk, utmost. Paper presented at the Pan-Canadian Education Research Agenda Symposium: Children and Youth at Risk, Ottawa, ON.

Mazurek, Kas & Winzer, Margret A. (Eds.) 1994. *Comparative studies in special education.* Gallaudet University Press: Washington, DC.

McLaughlin, M., Dyson, A., Nagle, K., Thurlow, M., Rouse, M., Hardman, M. et al. (2006). Cross-cultural perspectives on the classification of children with disabilities: Part II. Implementing classification systems in schools. *Journal of Special Education*, 40, 46 – 58.

Mitchell, David (Ed.) 2005. *Contextualizing inclusive education. Evaluating old and new international perspectives.* Routledge: New York, NY.

Moberg, S. & Savolainen, H. (2006). *Reading literacy and special education – The particular case of Finland.* In A. Lascioli & M. Onder (Eds.) Proceedings of the symposium on special pedagogy. State of the art in practical work, research and education (pp. 482 – 494). Verona: University of Verona.

OECD. (2004). Equity in education: Students with disabilities, learning difficulties and disadvantages – Statistics and Indicators. OECD: Paris.

OECD. (2007). PISA 2006. *Science competencies for tomorrow's world.* Volume 1 – Analysis. OECD: Paris.

OECD. (2009). Purchasing power parities (PPPs) for OECD countries. Retrieved October 28, 2009, from http://stats.oecd.org/Index. aspx?datasetcode=SNA_TABLE4

Powell, J.J.W. (2011). *Barriers to Inclusion. Special Education in the United States and Germany.* Paradigm Publisher: Boulder, CO.

Richardson, J.G. & Powell, J.J.W. (2011). *Comparing special education. Origins to contemporary paradoxes.* Stanford University Press: Stanford, CA.

Rytivaara, A., Pulkkinen, J. & Takala, M. (2012). Erityisopettajan työ: opettamista yksin ja yhdessä (The work of a special teacher: Teaching alone and together). In M. Jahnukainen (Ed.) Lasten erityishuolto ja –opetus Suomessa (The special care and education in Finland). 13th Ed. Tampere: Vastapaino, 333 – 352.

Sahlberg, P. (2007). Education policies for raising student learning: The Finnish approach." *Journal of Educational Policy,* 22, 147–171.

Sahlberg, P. (2009). *Learning first: School accountability for a sustainable society.* In K. Gariepy, B. Spencer and J-C Couture (Eds.) Educational Accountability. Professional Voices from the Field (pp. 1 – 22). Rotterdam/Boston/Taipei: Sense Publishers.

Simola, H. (2005). The Finnish miracle of PISA: Historical and sociological remarks on teaching and teacher education. *Comparative Education,* 41, 455-470.

Samoff, J. (2007). *Institutionalizing international influence.* In Arnove, R.F., Torres, C.A. & Franz, S. (Eds.) Comparative Education: The Dialectic of the Global and the Local, 52–91. Oxford: Rowman.

Statistics Finland (2010). Special Education. Helsinki: Tilastokeskus [Accessed: 28.11.2012] at http://www.stat.fi/til/erop/2010/erop_2010_2011-06-09_tau_005_fi.html

Välijärvi. J., Linnakylä, P., Kupari, P., Reinikainen, P. & Arffman, I. (2002). *The Finnish success in PISA – and some reasons behind it.* Jyväskylä: Kirjapaino Oma.

Wishart, D. & Jahnukainen, M. (2010). Difficulties associated with the coding and categorization of students with emotional and behavioural disabilities in Alberta. *Emotional and Behavioural Difficulties,* 15 (3), pp. 181–187.

Winzer, M. (2008). *Children with exceptionalities in Canadian classrooms*. 8th Ed. Toronto, ON: Pearson.

Chapter 6: The Level Playing Field – Unconcealing Diploma Exam Accommodation Policy[1]

W. John Williamson and W. James Paul

My first experience[2] with the concept of academic accommodation on diploma exams (mandatory exit exams Alberta's students are required to write) came 12 or so years ago when a colleague in counselling helped a student with a physical disability in my home-room group apply to Alberta Education for extended time on his upcoming diploma examinations. The physical disability was due to a genetic condition that had caused the congenital amputation of some of his fingers. His application was initially rejected because his diagnosis was too old. My colleague helped arrange for the student to see a physician who could verify that this condition was still disabling to the enterprise of writing, or, perhaps, we mused in sarcastic hyperbole, to verify that his lost fingers had not grown back since the last diagnosis. My colleague told me she was very tempted to send a picture along to accompany the more recent diagnosis in her letter of appeal.

In 2012, 55,361 diploma examinations were written by students completing Grade 12 courses in the province of Alberta. These standardized tests are weighted as 50% of the students' course grades in their Grade 12 core subjects – English Language Arts, Mathematics, Social Studies and the Sciences (Alberta Education, 2012). Alberta Education (2011) states the following reasons for these exams:

- To certify the level of individual student achievement in selected Grade 12 courses;

---

[1] This chapter first appeared in the *Journal of Applied Hermeneutics* October 30, 2012. Since its publication, a number of considerable improvements have been made to accommodations policy by Alberta Education. These are outlined at http://education.alberta.ca/admin/testing/diplomaexams/diplomabulletin.aspx

[2] This article contains frequent uses of experiential data written in the first person by the first author, John Williamson. For the sake of structural flow, we have chosen to use the first person voice throughout the piece, though we also want to emphasize that this work reflects the ideas and concerns of both authors.

- To ensure that province-wide standards of achievement are maintained; and

- To report individual and group results (p. 1).

Coming at the end of their high school careers, in courses that are required both for graduation from high school and, often, as prerequisites for post-secondary pathways students hope to embark on, these exams are the very epitome of "high-stakes testing".

For students who have been supported in the classroom through differentiated instruction, including students with diagnosed disabilities, the prospect of writing these standardized exams under rigidly controlled testing conditions is daunting. Focusing on some specific, diagnosable disabilities reveals some of the barriers to successful completion the exams would pose under regular conditions. For students with visual disabilities, standard print versions of the exams would obviously be inaccessible, but this is also true to some degree for students with diagnosed disabilities related to reading whose ability to interpret text would be hindered by their being asked to silently read some of the lengthy and complex exam booklets. The rigid time limits may also pose an unreasonable barrier for students with a variety of exceptionalities, including slow processing speeds, physical disabilities related to writing, mental health issues and Attention Deficit/Hyperactive Disorder (ADHD). These students need more time, either because it takes them longer to perform the academic tasks the exams required or because much of their writing time is inevitably lost to distraction or worry. The potential barriers that the standardized assessments under regular conditions pose to students with disabilities are a problem for the testers as well as the students. It is both an ethical concern in the sense that these barriers hinder the access to achievement opportunities for the students and a validity threat to anyone hoping to interpret data from these tests as they make it unclear whether a student's performance on a particular assessment represented his or her actual mastery of course outcomes or only a shadow of what he or she was capable of (Alberta Education, 2006; Webber, Aitken, Lupart, & Scott, 2009).

Alberta Education has formulated a comprehensive "response" system to address the potential barriers named above and to provide for reasonable accommodations for students writing diploma examinations to attempt to ensure that the diploma exams are administered equitably. This system is administered by the "Special Cases and Accommodations Division" of Alberta Education's Learner Assessment Branch. The concept of accommodation, as defined by Alberta Education, is important here. An Alberta Education (2006) "best learning practices" document entitled "Identifying Student Needs" defines accommodation as follows:

> An accommodation is a change or alteration in the regular way a student is expected to learn, complete assignments, or participate in classroom activities. Accommodations include special teaching or assessment strategies, equipment or other supports that remove, or at least lessen, the impact of a student's special education needs. The goal of accommodations is to give students with special education needs the same opportunity to succeed as other students (p. 1).

In the case of the Province of Alberta's diploma exams, accommodations are available to help ensure that students with disabilities are treated fairly and include the following:

- Audio CD versions of the exams;

- Extra writing time;

- A scribe to record student responses;

- Large-print versions of the exams;

- Braille versions of the exams

     (Alberta Education, 2011, p. 12).

The Special Cases and Accommodations Division, then, clearly articulate the principles that guide the provision of these learner accommodations claiming that:

> The goal of accommodation is not to optimize performance but to *level the playing field* (emphasis added) by removing obstacles to performance that are inequitable. Consequently, accommodations are neither intended nor permitted to:
>
> - Alter the nature of the construct being assessed by an examination;
>
> - Provide unfair advantage to students with disabilities or medical conditions over students taking examinations under regular standardized conditions, or compensate for knowledge or skill that the student has not attained (p. 12).

On this note, as illustrated in the anecdote at the start of this paper, the Special Cases and Accommodations Division require various forms of proof to legitimate the status of students as having a disability. Students with formal special education disability codes are required to document their codes and provide proof that they are consistently using the requested accommodations in classroom assessment. Students with disabilities not recorded in the Alberta Education coding system need to provide formal diagnoses and proof of consistent use of the accommodations (Alberta Education, 2011).

This approach seems thorough and balanced on a first reading. Students with disabilities are not patronized with excessive help and do not receive unfair advantages over other students. They are simply held accountable for demonstrating their knowledge of the curriculum through means appropriate to their diverse learning needs. I can speak to the tangible relief many students and teachers I work with seem to feel knowing that going into these important assessments, students writing diploma exams will have the use of the accommodations they require. I can also speak to the impressions I have gathered over years of practice as to the efficiency and consistency with which the Alberta Special Cases and Accommodations Division processes the accommodations applications and their willingness to work collaboratively when applications for accommodations were lacking. Instead of rejecting these applications with no chance of appeal, they have often worked patiently to help me properly document students' exceptionalities and proof of prior uses of accommodations so that many of the cases that were initially turned down were often eventually accepted. Within the closed system of their own rules and procedures, Special Cases and Accommodations Division often acts, from my observations, with professionalism, consistency, patience, and goodwill, and this work undoubtedly benefits many diverse learners facing these high-stakes tests.

As suggested in my example, however, despite the apparent successes I have encountered with this process of accommodation for diploma testing purposes, I have observed some problems as well. Students who are eligible to receive accommodations, and who I feel would clearly benefit due the difficulties they experience, often refuse them. They refuse accommodations actively by saying they are not interested or sometimes, it seems, they refuse accommodations more passively through persistent failure either to obtain the necessary signatures from parents and teachers or to turn in the sections of the applications they are responsible for in time to meet the provincial deadlines. Instead of being grateful for the accommodations, some coded students even seem resentful when I bring up the issues of their disabilities and the recommended accommodation for these disabilities, though, of course, I have no choice but to use disability labels. They are the currency required to obtain accommodations. The process of applying for accommodations is cumbersome, involving on my part, the distribution, completion, gathering and faxing of hundreds of pages of documentation to Special Cases and Accommodations every semester. Time I spend engaged in this enterprise is time taken away from directly helping students with disabilities and other struggling students with their coursework. Classroom teachers, who are an important part of the application team in the sense that they are required both to provide similar accommodations during classroom assessment and to work with the student to document the use of these accommodations, often seem resentful, too, not necessarily of accommodating the students but of the bureaucratic process.

Teachers who tend not to use strictly time-limited tests with students and/or who often read test questions out loud to students who are struggling to understand them are confused as to what constitutes a provable use of an accommodation in a diversified classroom where flexible assessment practices are neither formally announced as a departure from the norm nor limited to a limited set of eligible students, and the documents outlining the process of applying for accommodations (Alberta Education, 2011) provide no guidance on this. On the topic of eligibility, I often end up having to explain, with some difficultly, to students who are struggling in their classes and feel they might benefit from accommodations on their diploma exams, or teachers who are advocating for struggling students, why they too are not eligible for accommodations. Actually, to explain this question from the apparent perspective of Learner Assessment/Special cases is not difficult at all; for students with diagnosed disabilities, some aspects of the exams, such as time limits or the requirement to read silently, form unreasonable barriers that interfere with the assessment. For students deemed normal, even if they are struggling students who are thought normal, based only on a lack of a diagnosis to support the need for accommodation, the same aspects of the exam (silent reading, strict time limits) remain part of the curricular assessment and cannot be altered. Doing so would give them an unfair advantage over other students. This, however, is not an intuitively satisfactory explanation to offer to students, parents or teachers, and it starts to look even shakier if one questions the validity of educational labeling in the context of the ongoing controversies and definitional flux in the medical/psychological fields that inform the process (Aaron, 1997; Bienstock & Harper, 2011; Hacking, 1995; Klassen, 2002; Winzer, 2009). The claims to justice this policy makes also suffer whenever one simply wonders if there are, possibly, other ways of looking at the needs of struggling students than through the lens of disability (Clifford, Friesen, & Jardine, 2008; Jardine, 2012). These concerns all coalesce into the question of whether or not the current policies of accommodation do enough to make diploma examinations a just experience for students who require them in order to be fairly assessed by the exams.

A possible source of the resentment and confusion may have to do with a model/theory of disability that seems, quite clearly, to dominate the accommodations process but that has recently been frequently and openly challenged as an inappropriate way of interpreting disability or as a rubric to guide work with students with disabilities (Alberta Education, 2009; Dunn, 2010; Hibbs & Pothier, 2005). The individual deficit model that Special Cases and Accommodations Division continues to use to determine which students are suitable applicants for accommodations, while once the dominant discourse in special education (Winzer, 2009), has recently been criticized by stakeholders in special education as well as Disability Studies scholars as demeaning and exclusionary to individuals labeled as disabled and oblivious to the role of institutions in co-creating disabilities through exclusionary policy, stereotyping and the erection of unnecessary barriers (Danforth & Gabel, 2006; Dunn, 2010; Hibbs & Pothier, 2005). Critics note that despite the veneer of objectivity and scientific certainty with which documents such as the Diagnostic and Statistical Manual of Mental Disorders (Task Force for DSM IV, 2000) and educational documents such as the Alberta Special Education Coding Criteria manual (2010) describe disability as an individualized disorder, the social reality of disability is much more complicated than this.

Lest this concern seem excessively constructivist, it bears emphasizing that Disability Studies do not deny the reality that individuals have impairments that impact their lives, including their lives as students; rather, it sets out to critique what it claims to be dominant framings of these impairments as overarching, defining flaws or defects in individuals and the related social practices that disclose impairments through these negative framings (Hibbs & Pothier, 2005). It may be helpful to view this difference in perspectives hermeneutically, from a Heideggerian (1962) understanding of "unconcealment" as well. As Heidegger described in *Being and Time*, in a "clearing" (p. 133), a translator's footnote encourages us to understand this in a literal sense as a space in the woods offering apparently unobstructed visibility of a thing, a thing may well be unconcealed or revealed, but it still appears to us in a certain way that conceals other ways it may appear to us. In the "clearing" of the deficit model, in which people with disabilities have appeared or been disclosed as bearing individualized defects, "useful" technical knowledge has, admittedly, emerged about the nature of various impairments and about which accommodations might best assist people with these impairments. The enterprise of special education in general and, specific to this example, the process of diploma exam accommodation, depends on this knowledge (Alberta Education, 2006; Winzer, 2009). Other essential truths, however, are concealed by this disclosure. These include the phenomenon of the failure of institutions to be open, inclusive and convivial with a student who appears to learn differently as a result of individual defects solely lodged in the mind/body of the student (Hibbs & Pothier, 2005; Jardine, 2012).

The Level Playing Field

A closer examination of Special Cases and Accommodation's metaphor of the level playing field provides a hermeneutic un-concealing of the Alberta Education accommodation policy. Seeming ostensibly in this case to indicate the state of fair and reasonable competition where no advantage is granted to either side - "normal" or "disabled" learner - this phrase "level playing field" has been used so often in conversations about ensuring equal competitive opportunities in a variety of contexts that it is easy to overlook its various foundational assumptions and associations.

A very early use of the concept can be found in Christianity's Bible, in the following piece of tactical advice:

> And the servants of the king of Syria said unto him, their gods are gods of the hills; therefore they were stronger than we; but let us fight against them in the plain, and surely we shall be stronger than they (1 Kings 20:23, King James 2000 Version).

It is interesting to note that, in this quotation, the level playing field concept is not used as an invocation of fairness but as a strategic advantage that one side is seeking out over another in a test of even higher stakes than diploma exams, life and death combat. This meaning may linger as a reminder of the many ways this metaphor, which is now most often related to fairness, can still be used strategically. One might invoke ideas of fairness in order to gain advantage. Notwithstanding this possibility, the level playing field metaphor with its implied imagery of sporting competitions where the levelness of the playing surface is of importance tends to evoke notions of "fair play." It also suggests the expectation that fair play is ensured by some sort of outside arbiter, a referee of one kind or another to hold everyone playing accountable to standards of play. In some ways, this metaphor does speak powerfully to the desire of, and for, a marginalized person to be included equally with, but not patronized or given advantage over, the normative group from which he or she was originally set apart in some field of endeavour. A discourse of moderation towards the more privileged other reassures that the marginalized party is asking for no more than fairness. The applicability of this notion of "level playing field" needs to be questioned in the context of the sufficiency of accommodation policies in leveling the playing field that is the diploma exam experience.

"The Level Field?"

The first notion that might be highlighted lest the frequent use of this phrase dulls the senses is that, in the present context, it is a metaphor equating the imposition of high-stakes tests on students with competition in a rule-governed sport. The image of a field harkens to pastoral settings, in which members of a privileged leisure class partake in amateur sporting, such as games of croquet, cricket, or lawn bowling, or tennis. These participants attend in luxuriant solidarity to the rules of fair play that govern the gaming enterprise at play. Competition is rightful and worthwhile, and it is assumed with the willful naivety of class privilege that, even when the stakes are higher, the competition will be orderly and sporting. Still, despite the façade of fairness, the metaphor breaks down in a variety of ways when applied to high school high-stakes testing. First of all, aside from opting out of the widespread strong societal expectation of high school completion and, for many, the hope of advancing to some form of post-secondary education, the participants in this particular "educational sport" have no choice but to compete – and to compete well. More apt comparisons than gentle sporting might be made to the privileged spectator/coerced participant relationship in sports of kings such as horse racing or gladiatorial combat. Perhaps the recent dystopia novel and film, *The Hunger Games* (Collin, 2008), in which working class adolescents are compelled to partake in "to the death" combat for the entertainment of a privileged class might also be a better metaphor. While many would agree that competition is an integral aspect to the evolution of human experience, its value as a central theme of the educational enterprise is contestable. Discourses related to high-stakes testing that include "level playing field" uncritically advance competition, between students, between teachers and between school districts as an unequivocally positive phenomenon that will help ensure, in a (neo)classical liberal, capitalistic/marketing sense, quality education for all (Gorlewski, Porfilio, & Gorlewski, 2012; Graham & Neu, 2004; Kohn, 2000).

A Marxist reading of gladiatorial combat would point out that, other than earning the privilege to survive for another day, the gladiatorial combatant does not even really reap the fruits of his own victory. Similarly, while the diploma exam writer's transcript is certainly enhanced by a successful performance, these exams too speak of an alienation of labour. In terms of the exam as product, the student does not really choose to make it or how to make it, and the fruits of the academic labour are certainly used for a variety of purposes external to the student, involving larger "educational, economic and political establishments" (Garrison, 2012, p. 19). Admittedly, this Marxist critique of assessment has its limits. It is obviously standard practice for the teacher as practitioner/authority to assert some control over the types of tests and assignments the students produce, as well as to use the results of assessment for a variety of purposes related to instructional planning, communication, and placement (Webber et. al., 2009). In the case of diploma exams, however, the standardization of this control is well beyond the authority of the individual practitioner, and the totality of the appropriation of the student work does need to be questioned. The process is characterized by a de-humanizing surrender in which the students submit to the examiner, a "documentable" self, (Garrison, 2012) a surrender made all the more complete in the case of students with disabilities for whom this self is also documented as bearing deficits through the process of applying for accommodations. Once this machinery of sorting and objectification is unconcealed, the pastoral characterization of the level playing field again seems less fitting.

Level?

Though the process of diploma exam accommodations does not promise to make the entirety of the school experience equitable for students with disabilities, merely the summative exams, and the extent to which the larger playing field of public education may well continue to be tilted against students with disabilities bears comment. The exams do, after all, purport to test the success of these students in learning the larger Program of Studies. Despite a vast and comprehensive system of targeted support for students with disabilities (Alberta Education, 2004), systemically the rates of high school completion remain much lower for students with diagnosed disabilities than for students with no diagnoses. Specifically, according to Alberta Education's (2009) high school completion longitudinal study of the cohort of students who entered Grade 10 in 2002, 79.5% of the non-disabled students completed after three years but only 56.5% of students with mild to moderate disabilities and only 32.3% of students with severe disabilities were able to complete in the same amount of time. Though some of the same criticisms about flawed approaches to disability that I raise in this paper may apply to this apparent larger systemic failure to reach many of these learners in K-12 schooling, I only mention this concern in the context of the conversation about leveling the playing field of diploma examinations. Is it naivety or hubris to claim that the final test of a K-12 education that might have itself been inequitable for a student with a disability can really be made equitable by providing a few exam accommodations?

In the sense of the cliché that the tail of diploma examinations wags the dog of classroom instruction, the concern is that teacher anxiety over preparing students for diploma exams often results in "teaching to the test," or the use of superficial "drill and skill" teaching practices (Alberta Teachers' Association, 2009; Friesen, 2010; Kohn, 2000). This is particularly worrisome when it comes to students with disabilities. It has been argued that students with learning disabilities are especially in need of rich, varied, multi-sensory experiences with curriculum and assessment (Dunn, 2010; Jacobs & Dangling Fu, 2012), and they may suffer disproportionately in classrooms where repetitive, narrow forms of teaching and assessment that mirror the diploma exams themselves are used in misguided efforts to prepare students for their diploma examinations.

Returning to the issue of the diploma exams themselves, exams such as the English Language Arts diploma examinations for writing arguably only test about a third of the actual high school program of studies. While outcomes related to effective composition apply to both the larger program of studies and the exams, other writing outcomes such as "use process oriented writing strategies" seem to have been replaced with non-curricular outcomes such as, "generate ideas for writing quickly"; "produce a polished first draft"; and "write well under pressure" (Slomp, 2007, p. 184). Students with impairments related to spelling, writing, and anxiety while well-served by the generous, developmental, process-oriented approach to writing the program of studies for English endorses are hindered by the narrowed product-oriented understanding of writing diploma examinations impose. The playing field, again, may be tilted against students with disabilities in the excessive emphasis of these high-stakes assessments on curricular and even non-curricular outcomes with which they are likely to experience the most difficulty.

The power dynamics of accommodations policy too need to be questioned in the context of the plausibility of claims to levelness. Accommodations policies requiring extensive rules of application can, from a disability studies perspective, be understood as a bold exercise of institutional power and control on the self-identity of the individual with a disability (Hibbs & Pothier, 2005). The default position of the institution is to offer no accommodation and the general equity of the testing process for all is never up for debate. The student requiring the accommodation and the teachers facilitating the process are left with no choice but to endorse through their participation in the application process the institutional deficit-based understanding of disability and accept the rightfulness of the institutional approach to accommodation. Self-advocacy, understanding, and requesting the supports that one requires to learn successfully is a common theme in working with individuals with disabilities (Alberta Education, 2003). The only form of self-advocacy the accommodations process makes available is the docile (Foucault, 1977), self-application of a disability deficit label in order to be granted exceptional status.

Arbiters of Levelness

David Jardine (2008) shared the following ecological vision of a process of differentiation and accommodation that works in fundamentally different ways than that of the diploma exam accommodation process:

> *When I work in the garden with my seven-year-old son, I don't send him off to a "developmentally appropriate garden." I take him to the same garden where I am going to work. Now when we get there and get to the work that place needs, each of us will work, as each of us is able. We are not identical in experience, strength, patience and so on. But both of us will be working in the same place doing the real work that the garden requires (pp. 111-112).*

Consider how much attention, tact, and prudence on the part of a parent might be required to make working in a garden with a young child to be a pleasant experience for both parent and child. As new life is created in the garden by the work of the parent and child, significant learning is also occasioned by this practical activity. As part of this practical activity, the parent learns through conversing with and observing his child. He learns how much intervention is needed to ensure the child is able to make a real contribution to the enterprise, as an energetic seven year old would be able to with proper instruction, but s/he also learns how to foster the child's learning and enjoyment of gardening. He learns how much the child seems independently capable of and how much help he requires. Though the situation calls for reflection, it is a reflection grounded in solidarity and practical activity, in which the parent may intuitively grasp instead of reasoning out that the way to familiarize his son with the motion of raking the garden is by guiding his first strokes hand over hand until the child begins to master the motion. In this pedagogy, there is something of Heidegger's (1962) "ready to hand" imbedded understandings, like those of the master carpenters engaged in their trade.

The practicing teacher, like the parent in the example, instructs and assigns work and observes and talks to his or her students in order to decide how much assistance and support each student will require. I look, with gratitude, on the contributions the medical and psychological fields have made to teachers' understandings of which supports might prove most helpful for students with various impairments, but I feel these types of accommodations should always be grounded in the world of the teacher practitioner working with students. While it is helpful to understand why, from a medical/psychological perspective, a student may require more time than most, a wise teacher should not need a note from a psychologist to know better than to rip an assignment out of the hands of a student who is still actively engaged in completing it, possibly even learning something from the task. The wise teacher, when assisting a student who is having trouble comprehending a passage from a text, does not need clinical verification to know that one way to help might be to read the passage out loud to the student, lest some previously unnoticed aspect of the text announce itself to the student when additional senses are recruited in his or her effort to understand.

The medicalized individual deficit model, in its reliance on experts to declare which accommodations are legitimate for diploma exams, disrupts the "ready to hand" application of supportive pedagogy and alienates the teacher from the practical work of determining which supports his or her students require in the classroom in which they work together. Though it might be argued that there is some collaborative involvement of the classroom teacher in this process in that he or she is one of the signatories who must verify use of the accommodation in the classroom in order for the student to qualify, it bears asking, what exactly the classroom teacher is being asked to collaborate in? Does the signature of the classroom teacher help verify that it is abnormal for a teacher to offer, or a student to require, these forms of accommodation? Does it verify that the students who are well-served by these accommodations bear defects, and that the legal/clinical intervention of this document on classroom practice is welcome and necessary? The teacher who wants to see his or her students receive accommodation is coerced into being a witness, though not an expert witness, in the process, but is otherwise devalued by the requirement of additional medical/psychological verification on the part of a more "expert" witness.

The expert witness to the need for accommodation is the psychological or medical practitioner who, though he or she may have little or no actual experience working with the child as a learner, provides the documentation that confirms the disability status that makes available the accommodation. Writing of modernity's increased reliance on such experts when it comes to social determinations of import Gadamer (1992) wrote:

> Our society is not deformed just because experts are consulted and recognized for the superiority of their knowledge. Quite the opposite: It is almost a duty for human beings to incorporate as much knowledge as is possible in any of their decisions. Max Weber's famous expression "purposive rationality" [Zweckrationalität] applies here. For Weber demonstrated that there was a great danger implicit in those decisions which are determined by emotion or interest: In them the will to be rational is absent which would tie the attainability of the end to the rational determination of means. Max Weber saw a weakness in modern individualism because it permitted the subordination of the duty to know to the indeterminate authority of a good will, of a good intention, or of a pure conscience (pp. 188-189).

Who/What is this pure conscience? Any suggestion that the determinations of the types and levels of accommodation a student requires are messy, complicated and grounded not solely in clinical definitions but in lived experience in classrooms. This "messiness" would be antithetical to the quest for control and certainty that characterizes both the diploma exam experience proper (Graham & Neu, 2004) and its accommodation process (Hibbs & Pothier, 2005). Given this, the gatekeeper of such accommodation cannot be the student or the teacher, who are subjects being measured; it must come from the outside medical psychological expert and, ultimately, from the decision makers at Special Cases and Accommodations who evaluate these applications. Justice in the form of equitable treatment for the student does not emerge from within the messy solidarity in the work of learning in the classroom; it is administered prescriptively, from without by an outside, non-contaminated, medical/psychological authority. The referee or arbiter of the level playing field in this case is, in the Cartesian tradition, a curiously disembodied presence with no direct observational connection to the "game" being played and with often a fairly limited relationship to the participant requesting accommodation.

Play?

The presence of students using extra time can pose logistical difficulties in exam administration. As the students who qualified for extra time accommodation continued to write the morning examination well past 12:00 p.m., the exam administrator let students into the gymnasium for the afternoon exam and, once everyone was seated, proceeded to deliver instructions for the new exam over the microphone, all while the students receiving accommodations from the previous exam continue to write. On a different day, as the students who qualified for extra time continued to write the afternoon exam in their desks in the gymnasium, members of the basketball team began to, noisily, move the desks off to the side to make room for their evening practice.

In a shallowest sense that one type of "play" might be regulated activity like the basketball practice that began to happen during the exam, the characterization of the diploma examination as a form of "play," in the "level playing field" seems to apply. Gadamerian (2004) hermeneutics, however, reads play much more richly than this, as an experience of movement, freedom, sharing, and infinite, pleasurable regress. Play is the to and fro motion of a ball thrown in a game, or absent humans altogether, the play of light or the play of waves. In the shared project of meaning-making, play is how meaning is co-established, challenged, enriched, and re-established in conversation and, more broadly, in any interpretive activity. As a part of a festival, travelling players may put on a play in a small town and in a strange alchemy the original truth of the play is preserved even as each individual spectator interprets it according to his or her own horizons. The play of festive occasions or holidays, regular events of irregularity, suspends the ordinary relations to time, allowing time to tarry as members take stock of their lives and perhaps even take occasion to think of their lives differently. Though it seems to stretch plausibility to suggest that the diploma exam experience, or the diploma exam accommodation process have the potential to fully take on these richer forms of play, these understandings of play certainly point to how depressingly lacking "play" is in the playing field of diploma examinations.

Time to Play

If one is truly engaged in an academic subject, taking advantage of the opportunity to "tarry" (Jardine, 2008) over an important, summative academic task for that subject might be seen as an honouring of that subject, not a defect in the individual. Learner assessment's framing of this desire, however, echoes the concerns of the early 20th century managerial scientist Frederick Winslow Taylor (1911) that initiative and judgment about how to best perform a task, including how long it should take, is not the domain of the individual worker but the factory manager. In a managerial fetishization of baselines of normality, students are not even expected to do their best but to produce a baseline representation of their capabilities in a time-limited examination (Melnyck, 2012). Excellence is obtained through the managerial prodding of students and teachers towards ministry-set standards. No consideration is given to what conditions might actually inspire and enable students, as conscientious individuals, to craft their best work. This framing conceals wanting or needing extra time as conscientiousness and reveals it as an abnormality. In the rights of passage that saw apprentices go into seclusion to prepare the master crafts which would testify to their readiness for full membership in the guild (a tradition that is still carried on in academic rites of passage at the graduate level of post-secondary education), the mysteries of the discipline are honoured in the expectation that within generous, if any, time limits the candidates will produce their best work (Rutherford, 1987). In the diploma exam milieu, the framing of "extra time" through the deficit model and the sense of the students work as a baseline sample strips both the students and the occasion itself of the dignity that might otherwise arise out of their diligent effort during this summative gathering in the name of the academic discipline.

Framing it as *abnormal* to need or want more time invites interpretations of students as *others*, for which normal expectations of care, tact, and civility need not apply. The accommodation of twice the writing time may render the examination an excessively grueling experience. In such a case, the students' optimal levels of concentration and focusing abilities are exhausted long before the provided time is. The validity of tests to measure academic achievement is considered to be reduced if the examinations are too long (Topper, 2001). If, as a thought experiment, examinations for non-accommodated students were deemed to be insufficiently comprehensive and subsequently lengthened and scheduled for a writing time of five or six consecutive hours instead of the current two to three hours, one could imagine students, parents, teachers and other stakeholders in education complaining vociferously that this increase in testing time was not only a threat to the examination validity and reliability, but a cruel and unusual imposition on students. Basically then, a length of test-taking time that would, hypothetically, be deemed Draconian for non-accommodated students is offered as a fairness provision for an accommodated student, despite the fact that there is no indication that processing information more slowly increases one's stamina for intellectual activities or reduces one's vulnerability to fatigue. Are these slower-working students deemed to be super-human in their ability to withstand lengthy examinations?

Does learner assessment's parsimonious approach to the time accommodation "problem" trickle down to schools? It provokes suspicion as to whether the students truly need or deserve this time provision or if they are in fact playing the system and loitering. On an institutional level, are Alberta's accommodated students, past the end of the scheduled writing time for other students, given the same right to a silent and distraction-free writing centre, or as the examination winds down, do they begin to be treated, in some schools, as academic loiterers? In addition to the aforementioned examples in my anecdote, I have observed announcements being made to extra time students, near the end of their allotted additional time that they had "30 minutes left" and if they were not finished by then it was "too bad", and I have wondered if this same stern warning would have been given near the end of the "normal" amount of writing time to the larger body of "normal" students still gathered. In order to, understandably, keep writing centres orderly and distraction-free, exam administrators often regulate no food or drink policies. Is it fair that students writing for five hours instead of three be held to these policies? Does this encourage a system where exam supervisors eager to finally be released from the shifts they hoped would only last three hours repeatedly ask accommodated students if they are "done yet"?

Leveling for Otherness

- Accommodations are neither intended nor permitted to provide unfair advantage to students with disabilities or medical conditions. (Alberta Education, 20112).

- Whatever you do, whichever battle you fight, whichever course of action you attempt, with what are you going to inform it all? The love of difference or the passion for similarity? The former – especially if it becomes socially contagious (through education, cultural action, political action) – leads to human life. The latter leads, in full-blown or latent form, to exploitation, repression, sacrifice, rejection. Yes or no, can we live together in fundamental mutual recognition, or must we exclude one another? (Stiker, 1999, p. 11).

A colleague was assisting me in helping a group of students with diagnosed disabilities, in this case mostly made up of students with learning disabilities and behavioural / emotional disabilities, in the application process for accommodations on diploma examinations. He told the students, "It is really important that you advocate for yourselves by asking for accommodations because you look so normal. When people see you they can't tell anything is wrong with you."

Stiker presented the choice between love of difference and the passion for similarity as binaries and, in the interest of social justice; they are well considered this way. It seems, however, these differences sometimes blend into each other as well. "Accommodation", for example, in the less clinical sense means that which fulfills our most familiar needs such as those for food or lodging, but it can also be defined as something that is granted, given up, or even sacrificed in negotiations between parties (Oxford Dictionaries, 2012). In *Strangers, Gods and Monsters*, Kearney's (2003) insightful hermeneutic reading of these three eponymous interpretive alternatives to otherness in which the author, with some help from Derrida, emphasized the slipperiness of hospitable acts such as accommodation when he wrote:

> Derrida has much to say about such alien matters in *On Hospitality*. Generally understood the subject of hospitality is a generous host who decides as a master chez lui, who to invite into his home. But it is precisely because of such sovereign self-possession that the host comes to fear certain others who threaten to invade his house, transforming him from a host into a hostage. The laws of hospitality thus reserve the right of each host to evaluate, select and choose those he/she wishes to include or exclude; that is the right to discriminate. Such discrimination requires that each visitor identifies him or herself before entering one's home. And this identification process indispensable to the 'law of hospitality' (hospitalité en droit) – involves at least some degree of violence (p. 69).

The relative strangeness of these others, in this case, accommodated-for students, is reinforced by the ongoing norm-based discourses which themselves cast the "accommodated other" as the departure from the norm. These concerns have historically and continue to infuse public education, in particular thinking about students with disabilities (Graham & Slee, 2005). Kearney (2003) identified strangers as a limit-experience to us "relatively normals" in that they challenge us to identify ourselves over and against others and, he noted, monsters pose an even stronger limit-experience in reminding us that the self is never quite safe, sovereign, or secure. This is a constant "there but for the grace of God go I" moment.

All of these anxieties resonate within the policy document from Special Cases and Accommodation Division (Alberta Education, 2011). Even as this document grants under what conditions a student might qualify for testing accommodations, it also delineates when the accommodations will be refused. Even as this document advances its reified notion of fairness for the accommodated student, it spells out its limits, sternly warning that no advantage will be given – the rules are sacrosanct. The rules and procedures, and the abuses that would constitute a breach of these rules, are minutely described for every believed necessary accommodation. The other, a contrived but seemingly necessary stranger or monster, self-identifies and he/she is invited into the "house" that is the institutional event of the diploma examinations. Does the anxious host take hostages when these guests are judged to be a threat to the façade of fairness and openness that "all" guests – it is claimed by the house – have access to? Like Kearney/Derrida's "anxious host," the testers know their obligations to these identifiable others but remain anxious. Their hospitality is immediately tinged with a jealous protectiveness of the center, or the norm, or the proper and good. Still, what is there to protect? Perhaps it is test security, precision of measurement, application rigour, observable governability and, above all, the reified concept of an equitable and equal level playing field of competition.

Disability rights have been hard won through a combination of the activism of people with disabilities and their supporters and legal challenges (Hibbs & Pothier, 2005; Shannon, 2011, Zelma, 2009). Still, despite public claims from institutions that their responses to this activism are well-intended, they have often been characterized by "stubborn reluctance" (Shannon, 2011, para. 1) or through institutional nods to public pressure more so than to clear commitments to inclusive policy (Hibbs & Potheir, 2005). This creates, at times, a tense relationship in which the rights-based discourse of people with disabilities and their supporters is met with a stern regulatory discourse on the part of the educational institution. Policy makers in the educational institution spell out a regulatory process of application for accommodation that is more reflective of fear of legal action than of deeply held commitments to inclusion. Under a deficit-based system where accommodations are only granted to those who are deemed categorically eligible, detailed written policy about how to seek accommodations becomes obviously necessary. The tone of such instruction, however, is often less than welcoming, and a discursive shift often takes place in which the policy moves from describing how to apply for accommodations to a legalistic listing of the limits to accommodation and the failures on the part of the applicant that will result in ineligibility (Hibbs & Pothier, 2005). In the Albertan diploma exam milieu, the Special Case Division's written requirements sometimes take on this officious tone. The intent is not to give "advantage" or "optimize performance" (Alberta Education, 2011, p. 12) the documents caution, casting students with disabilities as potential cheats at the outset of the process. Moreover, if the stringent documentation requirements, deadlines, and necessary signatures are not fully provided on the accommodations applications, "Special Cases and Accommodations will not approve [the] applications" (Alberta Education, 2011, p. 16.). Writing similar concerns about the rigidity of policy, demeaning reliance on deficit understanding of disability, and insistence on individual exceptional accommodation instead of broad institutional action towards inclusiveness students with disabilities at the post-secondary level face, Hibbs and Pothier (2005,) provocatively title a book chapter "Mining a level playing field or playing in a minefield?"

Alternatives

"I am convinced that even in a highly bureaucratized, thoroughly organized and thoroughly specialized society, it is possible to strengthen existing solidarities. Our public life appears, to me, to be defective in so far as there is too much emphasis upon the different and disputed, upon that which is contested or in doubt. What we truly have in common and what unites us thus remains, so to speak, without a voice. Probably we are harvesting the fruits of a long training in the perception of differences and in the sensibility demanded by it. Our historical education aims in this direction, our political habits permit confrontations and the bellicose attitude to become commonplace. In my view, we could only gain by contemplating the deep solidarities underlying all norms of human life." (Gadamer, 1992, p. 192).

I do not wish to simply raise a series of concerns about Alberta's diploma exam accommodations without suggesting interpretive and practical alternatives that might move the processes forward towards a more inclusion-based vision of diversity. It is through ongoing dialogue and keeping things in the realm of possibility that we are best able to treat students as students, not as reified groups and, in doing so, strive toward more just policies and practices. It is fair to say that it is possible that educators have only begun to understand some of the institutional barriers many students face, our very definitions about who does or does not have educational disabilities are problematic, and that the current process of accommodations does not live up to the claim that it addresses issues of fairness for all students with disabilities. This is a significant minority of students often considered to be especially vulnerable to some of the negative consequences of high-stakes testing (ATA, 2009; Gorlewski et al., 2012, Katsyannis et al., 2007, Lin, 2009). If, therefore, there are problems ensuring fairness through accommodation, perhaps the fairest measure to accommodate for disabilities would be to discontinue diploma examinations for all students. When it comes to students with disabilities, and possibly all students, high-stakes tests may measure too narrowly, weigh too heavily, provoke unnecessary anxiety, evoke test disability instead of ability, accommodate too stingily and essentially work to hinder the right of the student to a rich, fair, and sound educational experience (Disability Rights Advocates, 2001; Katsyannis et al., 2007).

In light of current Alberta Premier Allison Redford's and her former Minister of Education's recent statements questioning the high weighting of these exams and the controversies surrounding the effect of diploma examinations on the national competitiveness of Alberta's students in terms of securing post-secondary scholarships and admission based on marks requirements (Calgary Association of Parents and School Councils, 2011), the suggestion that they be discontinued, while unlikely even under this regime, seems a little less unthinkable. Even the proposed changes of the weighting of exams, from 50% to 25% of the students' final grades, while not eliminating any of the issues I have mentioned, might at least help on the level of harm reduction by lowering the stakes. In this vein, an extensive literature review of high-stakes testing and students with disabilities in American schools (Katsyannis et al., 2007) recommends that states that insist on using high-stakes testing best level the playing field for students with disabilities and all students by "making high school graduation decisions based on multiple indicators of students' learning and skills" (p. 166). Certainly in the Alberta system, lowering the weight of this one controversial indicator would make greater space for other measures of student achievement.

It seems unwise, however, to discuss pedagogic concerns such as these with "an all or none" approach when prudent educational researchers in Alberta and other districts where high-stakes testing is used often accept it as not so much desirable, but as present for the time being, and choose to discuss good pedagogy under these conditions (Friesen, 2010; Gorlewski et al., 2012). Though the Alberta Teachers' Association has never withdrawn its original objections to the use of high-stakes tests for grading students, it also remains engaged with Alberta Education as a participant in the discussion of how to make the tests as fair as possible for as long as they exist (ATA, 2009). Many students are presently impacted by these tests and related accommodation policies and we wish, therefore, to address the possibilities for a more just system of accommodation within the present reality of diploma testing. Though this suggestion may at first seem at odds with the historical and inspiring struggle for equal rights for individuals with disabilities to achieve a "level playing field," perhaps the notions of precisely quantifiable "equity" and "advantage" in terms of many of the accommodations more commonly offered needs to be revisited in light of the possibly more appropriate concepts named by disability studies scholars, Hibbs and Pothier (2005), as accommodation within the standard and flexibility for all. This paradigm aims to make general instruction and assessment as accessible as possible instead of relying on a model of "individual exception to the general standard" (p. 199) and is, in fact, the model of accommodation the Supreme Court of Canada recommends as the starting point for human rights legislation. Speaking of university assessment, Hibbs and Pothier offered the example of how, instead of accommodating for the many types of disabilities that render time-limited tests inaccessible through individual exception, using take-home tests whenever possible provides the same accommodation more democratically, and without reliance on deficit labeling. While it is difficult to imagine take-home diploma accommodations, this vision does inspire speculation of practical application of these principles to diploma testing. With the rapid growth of accessibility technologies, any PC or Mac user can now access features on standard software to read text out loud and can dictate orally to a computer that will translate his or her speech to text. With the passing of distracted driving legislation in Alberta, which bans manual operation of Smart phones and cellular phones while driving, many multi-tasking drivers are using hands-free, voice activated technologies, which are legally sanctioned as less impairing than hand-held devices under the new legislation. Understanding technological supports such as speech to text and text to speech through the lens of disability accommodation is becoming increasingly antiquated. Alberta Education's Special Cases and Accommodations Division has worked very hard to ensure that no accommodations pose a validity threat to the "constructs" of the diploma examinations, so framing reading and writing options for all to include broadly optional audio CDs and use of speech to text software would be no real threat. "Broadening [these] definitions of reading [and] writing" for all students (Dunn, 2010, p. 18; see also Edyburn, 2009) would not only eliminate an unnecessarily negative framing of impairments that impact reading and writing, it might grant many more students not an advantage, but a more flexible means to show their competencies. Though this might be seen as undermining the importance of more primary, physical reading and writing skills, these things are still relatively ubiquitous in K-12 education and broadening the technological options students have to interpret the complex texts and produce the complex responses the examinations require seems unlikely to contribute to producing a generation of non-readers/writers. Opening up these options might be seen as a stance towards emerging technologies equivalent to Alberta Education's eventual support of widespread use of word processing as an option for completing the written portions of diploma examinations. While at one time, almost all students in Alberta wrote diploma exams using pen and paper (Hart, 1987) and many states and provinces still allow word processing only as a special education accommodation (Katsyannis et al., 2006; Lin, 2010), Alberta Education now makes this accommodation broadly available, and their records indicate 80% of Alberta's students selected this technology for producing written responses on diploma exams last year (Alberta Education, 2012). We do not suggest that 80% of students may eventually choose to listen to the readings and dictate their responses on diploma exams, only that these options now broadly available on standard computing software should, like the option of word processing, be made available to any students who would choose to use them. As well, the issue of time needs to be revisited. When avoiding an individual deficit interpretation that sees the need for "extra" time as abnormal, the presence of a significant minority of students who seem to require more than the allotted three hours can re-emerge, unconcealed, as a problem with the length of the assessments in general. This unconcealing may lead to learner assessment reconsidering the length of the exams for all learners.

Reframing these reading, writing, and time accommodations to allow for more flexible assessment conditions for all students would, for many students with disabilities, strip the layer of "governance of disability" (Tremain, 2005) from the diploma testing experience. There would no longer be the need to self-identify, given the broad availability of what were formerly accommodations. The application process for remaining accommodations, Braille, and large-print exams, for example, obvious in their specificity to discreet impairments, might be streamlined to meet the logistical needs of ordering more so than the complex burden of proof of disability and prior usage of the accommodations.

I remain doubtful about whether diploma exams proper are an educational practice that is consistent with the values of inclusive education, or to put it another way: I question if underlying technologies of control, surveillance, and competition are things to which any student, least of all more vulnerable students, should be subject. Still, if diploma exams are to remain, for now, as highly weighted academic tasks students are required to complete in order to graduate, ongoing critique is needed to ensure their consistency with the educational values of inclusive education the larger institution of Alberta Education purports to hold. Significant re-design of the accommodations process and examination design and administration may help push diploma examination policy out of the individual deficit model and at least provide all students with greater access to, in the words of Foucault (1988) various "technologies of the self" to select their preferred options for responding to the assessments, thereby mitigating, at least to some degree, that impact of the larger "technologies of power" that characterizes the whole enterprise.

Acknowledgement

I (John Williamson) would like to gratefully acknowledge the mentorship of Dr. Jim Field, who has engaged me in conversations about justice for students when he taught me as an undergraduate, and then again during my M.A., and as he now continues to teach me as my PhD supervisor. This article would not be possible without the seeds of thought and concern these conversations planted in me.

References

Aaron, P. (1997). The impending demise of the discrepancy formula. *Review of Educational Research*, 67, 461 - 502. DOI: 10.3102/00346543067004461

Alberta Education. (2012). Accountability pillar results for annual education results report (AERR). Edmonton, AB: Government of Alberta.

Alberta Education. (2012). High school completion in Alberta. Edmonton, AB: Government of Alberta. http://education.alberta.ca/admin/highschoolcompletion/albertacompletion rate.aspx

Alberta Education. (2012). Department information and newsroom. Retrieved from *Inclusive Education*: http://education.alberta.ca/department/ipr/inclusion.aspx

Alberta Education. (2011). *Diploma examinations: Frequently asked questions*. Edmonton, AB: Government of Alberta.

Alberta Education. (2011). General information bulletin diploma examination program. Edmonton, AB: Government of Alberta.

Alberta Education. (2011). Special education. Retrieved from special education statistics: Alberta Education. (2010). Special Education Coding Criteria. Edmonton, AB: Government of Alberta.

Alberta Education. (2009). Setting the direction: Framework. Edmonton, AB: Government of Alberta.

Alberta Education. (2009). Accountability and reporting division high school completion longitudinal study. Edmonton, AB: Crown in Right of Alberta.

Alberta Education. (2006). Identifying student needs: Selecting accommodations and strategies. Edmonton, AB: Government of Alberta.

Alberta Education. (2004). Standards for special education. Edmonton, AB: Crown in Right of Alberta.

Alberta Education. (2003). Unlocking potential: Key components of programming for students with learning disabilities. Edmonton, AB: Crown in Right of Alberta.

Alberta Teachers' Association. (2009). *Real learning first: The teaching profession's view of student assessment.* Edmonton, AB: Government of Alberta.

Allan, J. (2008). *Rethinking of inclusive education: The philosophers of difference in practice.* Dorecht, The Netherlands: Springer.

Bienstock, R. (Producer), & Harper, S. (Director). (2011). The age of anxiety [Motion Picture]. Canada: Canadian Broadcasting Corporation.

Calgary Association of Parents and School Councils. (2011). CAPSC question for parents and school councils. Calgary, AB: Government of Alberta. Retrieved from http://www.capsc.ca/site/story.asp?id=531&tactic=38

Clifford. P., Friesen, S. & Jardine. D.W. (2008). *Whatever happens to him happens to us: Reading coyote and reading the world.* In D.W. Jardine, P. Clifford, & S. Friesen (Eds.), *Back to the basics of teaching and learning Thinking the World Together,* (pp. 67-78). New York, NY: Routledge.

Collins, S. (2008). *The Hunger Games.* New York, NY: Scholastic.

Danforth, S., & Gabel, S. (2006). *Vital questions facing disability studies in education.* New York, NY: Peter Lang.

Disability Rights Advocates. (2001). Do no harm-high-stakes testing and students with learning disabilities. Retrieved from www.dralegal.org/downloads/pubs/do_no_har m.pdf

Dunn, P. (2010). ReSeeing (Dis)ability. In Dudley-Marling, C., & Gurn, A. (Eds) (2010). *The Myth of the Normalcy Curve.* New York, NY: Peter Lang. Originally published in *English Journal,* (2010 November) Volume 100, pp. 14-26.

Edyburn, D. (2009). Principles of universal design and the implications for policy initiatives. Retrieved from www.education. alberta.ca/media/938200/edyburnudlreport.pdfStatistics, Courses Information Sheet. Retrieved from http://math. ucalgary.ca/files/math/ courses/F09/AMAT217/lec6/AMAT217-F09- LEC6-outline.pdf

Foucault, M. (1988). *The means of correct training.* In P. Rabinow (Ed.), *The Foucault reader* (pp. 188-205). New York, NY: Pantheon.

Foucault, M. (1977). *Discipline and punish.* (A. Sheridan, Trans.). New York, NY: Vintage.

Foucault, M. (1988). In L. Martin, H. Gutman, & P. Hutton (Eds.), *Technologies of the self.* Boston, MA: University of Massachusetts.

Friesen, S. (2010). Uncomfortable bedfellows: Discipline based inquiry and standardized examinations. *Teacher Librarian,* 37(6), 8-14.

Gadamer, H.G. (1992). *The limitations of the expert.* In D. Misgeld & G. Nicholson (Eds.), *Hans-Georg Gadamer on education, poetry, and history* (L. Schmidt & M. Reuss, Trans.) (pp. 165-181). New York, NY: State University of New York.

Gadamer, H.G. (2004). *Truth and method* (J. Weinsheimer, & D.G. Marshall, Trans.) London, England: Continuum.

Gallagher, D. (2010). *Educational research and the making of normal people.* In C. Dudley-Marling & A. Gurn (Eds.). *The myth of the normal curve,* (pp. 25-39). New York, NY: Peter Lang.

Garrison, J. (2012). *Academic labour as alienated labour: Resisting standardized testing.* In J. Gorlewski, B. Porfilio, & D. Gorlewski (Eds.). *Using high-stakes testing for students: Exploiting power with critical pedagogy.* New York, NY: Peter Lang.

Gorlewski, J., Porfilio, B., & Gorlewski, D. (2012). *Introduction.* In J. Gorlewski, B. Porfilio, & D. Gorlewski (Eds.). *Using high-stakes testing for students: Exploiting power with critical pedagogy.* New York, NY: Peter Lang.

Graham, C., & Neu, D. (2004). Standardized testing and the construction of governable persons. *Journal of Curriculum Studies,* 36(3), 295-319. DOI: 10.1080/0022027032000167080

Hacking, I. (1995). *Rewriting the soul: Multiple personality and the sciences of memory.* New Jersey, NY: Princeton.

Hart, L.C. (1987). Teaching high school English with Alberta's diploma exams: An assessment through oral research and dramatic presentation. MEd. project, University of Lethbridge, Lethbridge, AB. Retrieved from https://www.uleth.ca/dspace/handle/10133/110

Heidegger, M. (1962). *Being and time.* (J. Macquarrie & E. Robinson, Trans.). New York, NY: Harper Collins.

Hibbs, T., & Pothier, D. (2005). *Post-secondary education and disabled students: Mining a level playing field or playing in a minefield?* In D. Pothier & R. Devlin (Eds.), Critical disability theory: Essays in philosophy, politics, policy, and law (pp. 195-222). Vancouver, BC: UBC Press.

Jardine, D.W. (2012). The Descartes lecture. *Journal of Applied Hermeneutics*, Article 7. PID: http://hdl.handle.net/10515/sy5pr7n88.

Jardine, D.W. (2008). *Because it shows us the way at night: On animism, writing, and the re-animation of Piagetian theory.* In D.W. Jardine, P. Clifford, & Friesen (Eds.). Back to the basics of teaching and learning: Thinking the world together (pp. 105-116). New York, NY: Routledge.

Jardine, D.W. (2008). On the while of things. *Journal of the American Association for the Advancement of Curriculum Studies*, 4. Retrieved from ww2.uwstout.edu/content/ jaaacs/vol4/jardine.pdf

Katsyannis, A., Zhang, D., Ryan, J., & Jones, J. (2007). High-stakes testing and students with disabilities: Challenges and promises. *Journal of Disability Policy Studies*, 18, 160-167. DOI: 10.1177/10442073070180030401

Kohn, A. (2000). Standardized testing and its victims. *Education Week*. Sept. 27, 2000. Retrieved from: EducationWeek-file:///Macintosh%20HD/Desktop%20Folder/ew_printstory.cfm

Klassen, R. (2002). The changing landscape of learning disabilities in Canada 1989 - 2000. *School Psychology International*, 23, 199-219.

Lin, P-Y. (2010). Test accommodations in Canadian provincial assessments. Retrieved from Canadian Test Centre: www.canadiantestcentre.com

Oxford Dictionaries On-Line (2012). Retrieved from http://oxforddictionaries.com/

Redi, D., & Valle, J. (2001). The discursive practice of learning disability: Implications for instruction and parent-school relations. *Journal of Learning Disabilities,* 37, 466-481. DOI: 10.1177/00222194040370060101

Rutherford, E. (1987). *Sarum: A novel of England*. New York, NY: Random House.

Sands, A. (2013). Major changes planned for Alberta school achievement tests. *The Edmonton Journal*. http://www.edmontonjournal.com/news/Major+changes+planned+Alberta+school+achievement+tests/8361594/story.html

Shakespeare, T.A. (2002). The social model of disability: An outdated ideology? Research in Social Science and Disability, 2, 9-28.

Shannon, J. (2011). The promised land will be wheelchair accessible. *Chicago Sun Times*. Retrieved from http://blogs.suntimes.com/demand/2011/10/the_promised_ land_will_be_wheelchair-accessible.html

Simons, M., & Masschelein, J. (2005). *Inclusive education for exclusive pupils*. In S. Tremain (Ed.), Foucault and the Government of Disability (pp. 208-297). Ann Arbour, MI: University of Michigan Press.

Slee, R., & Allan, J. (2001). Excluding the included: A recognition of inclusive education. *International Studies in Sociology of Education*, 11(2), 173-191.

Slomp, D. (2007). *Trapped between paradigms: Composition pedagogy in the context of a twelfth grade standardized writing assessment*. [Electronic Version]. ProQuest – Dissertations & Theses. Edmonton, AB: University of Alberta.

Stiker, H.J. (2002). *A history of disability*. (W. Sayer, Trans.) Ann Arbor, MI: University of Michigan.

Task Force on DSM IV. (2000). Diagnostic and statistical manual of mental disorders (4th ed. rev.). Washington, DC: *American Psychiatric Association*.

Taylor, F.W. (1911). The principles of scientific management. Retrieved from http://www.marxists.org/reference/subject/economics/taylor/principles/index.htm

Topper, D. (2001). Examining the motives behind standardized tests. *Social Education*, Sept. 2001.

Tremain, S. (Ed.) (2005). *Foucault and the government of disability*. Ann Arbour, MI: University of Michigan Press.

Webber, N., Aitken, N., Lupart, J., & Scott, S. (2009). The Alberta Student Assessment Study: Final report. Edmonton, AB: Crown in Right of Alberta.

Zelma, G. (2009). Leveling the playing field - Special Education and the Law. NYU Child Study Centre. Retrieved from http://www.aboutourids.org/articles/understanding_special_education_law

Epilogue: Equity in Alberta Schools – 'So far from home'?

Stephen Murgatroyd, PhD FRSA FBPsS and J-C Couture, PhD

The challenges of addressing equity and assuring the well-being of Alberta's children and youth point to the broader systemic issues facing our increasingly volatile and complex human relationships globally. This was a theme explored by Margaret Wheatley in a public lecture Alberta: *So far from home? Creating vibrant communities for schools in the next Alberta*, November 29, 2012 in Edmonton.

The evening conversation, sponsored by the Alberta Teachers' Association and facilitated by Stephen Murgatroyd, had much to say about our need to rekindle our commitment to the well-being of children and youth. As Wheatley observed, Alberta is currently a place of stark contrasts. The paradoxes and promises of the challenges we face in our communities are apparent on a number of levels:

- Schools are the hubs of vibrant communities, yet are we committed to sustaining them?

- We are the some of the richest people on the planet, yet one out 12 Alberta children lives in poverty.

- Alberta's booming population is growing in diversity; yet we remain ambivalent about what we mean by "community".

- Amidst our economic growth, viable communities and neighbourhoods must be sustained in the face of threats such as urban sprawl and environmental degradation.

The current young generation of Albertans is growing up in the context of a booming province which is becoming increasingly diverse and is expected to reach five million by 2020. Our cities of tomorrow will struggle to avoid social fragmentation while rural communities will remain the same size or decline.

As a community 'imagineer', Wheatley raised some provocative reflections on the current malaise of our social and individual well-being. First and foremost as a community organizer, she reminds marginalized and disenfranchised groups that "no one is coming to help them", yet they have tremendous power "in and through community". She suspects that this applies to us here in Alberta. Certainly if we are to engage the well-being of children and youth, we need to be mindful that no one is coming to resolve this issue for us.

Her newest book - *So Far from Home: Lost and Found in Our Brave New World* (Berrett-Koehler, San Francisco, 2012) - feels dark. When asked why by the forum participants, she quietly replied that "these are dark times". During the evening talk, she catalogued the shadows and curtains on our world, including the sense that the problems we face are increasing and the solutions we try do not appear to work; we appear to have shrinking resources as we expand our presence on the planet, but no means of increasing our ability to supply food, water and energy equitably; individuals feel an increasing uncertainty about their identity and the meaning of their lives, yet they are better connected through technology with other voices than they have ever been; people report that they are "busy, busy, busy" and that they are overwhelmed and experience fear, anxiety and distress.

Wheatley reminded the audience that "nothing living lives alone" and that "we are bundles of potential that manifests only in relationship". So as to create health and move to solutions, we need to make connections and build community. Given that, in her view, "no one else is coming", it is critical to realize that, in the words of the Native American Hopi Elders, "we are the ones we have been waiting for".

Becoming "Warriors" for Alberta's Children

Margaret Wheatley reminds us that leadership both individually and in a community is standing up for what you care about.

As the contributors to this book illustrate, if we are to pursue equity, we do not need a "hero" leader or a group of leaders within the community. Life is connected, and it does not rest on one person, a hero, or one group. It is about all of us coming together to discover life's simultaneously subtle but simple – cruel but beautiful– realities. Pursuing social justice is not difficult but rather an intentional "being in the present" with one another that will have great impact in our communities. We do not exist alone, and we share basic human needs.

We need to work together to develop our capacity to engage in deep and respectful listening. This will enable us to build great community. We have to create conditions where people can come together to have courageous conversations about the things that matter. In Wheatley's view, we must become "warriors for the human spirit".

On a practical level, what might this look like? For the past year, the Association has outlined a comprehensive agenda for transforming Alberta's schools. An integral part of this agenda is immediate and long term actions outlined in *A Great School for All – Transforming Education in Alberta*. These include recognizing the following three principles and priorities in order to address our current shortcomings:

1. **Early learning is the cornerstone of Alberta's future.**

   From March 2012 to April 2013, Alberta's 42 women's shelters had to turn away 15, 032 women along with their 12,881 children (Alberta Council of Women's Shelters, 2013). Resource-rich Alberta ranked second last on the most recent national comparison of early education services across Canada. The independent report ranked provinces on 15 benchmarks associated with the delivery of high-quality early childhood programs. The benchmarks were organized into five categories: governance, funding, access, learning environment and accountability. Alberta scored three out of a possible 15 points. Quebec, which received 10 points, was the most highly rated province (McCain, Mustard and McCuaig 2011).

2. **Equity is the cornerstone on the path to excellence and economic competitiveness.**

   Early-learning and ongoing education programs help children to realize their full potential and lead more productive and fulfilling lives. They also significantly reduce the amount that governments would otherwise spend on justice, health, welfare and correctional programs. There is a growing consensus among economists and sociologists that high-quality early childhood development programs may in fact be good "investments" that have long-term economic returns ranging from $7 to $17 for every dollar invested in such programs (Schweinhart and Weikart 1993).

3. **Strong communities will foster vibrant children and youth.**

   Working with education partners, the Alberta Education should initiate pilot programs to implement the ground-breaking memorandum of agreement between the Government of Canada, the Government of Alberta and the Assembly of Treaty Chiefs of Alberta. This agreement is the foundation for enhancing learning for First Nations students (Government of Canada 2010).

In closing her presentation, Wheatley drew attention to the prophecies of the Hopi Nation – an Arizona American First Nation that captures both our imagination and the courage it will take to act in order to become warriors for Alberta's children and youth.

This could be a good time!

There is a river flowing now very fast.

It is so great and swift that there are those who will be afraid.

They will try to hold on to the shore.

They will feel they are being torn apart, and they will suffer greatly.

Know the river has its destination.

The elders say we must let go of the shore, push off into the middle of the river, keep our eyes open, and our heads above the water.

See who is there with you and celebrate.

At this time in history, we are to take nothing personally.

Least of all ourselves.

For the moment that we do, our spiritual health and journey comes to a halt.

The time of the lone wolf is over. Gather yourselves!

Banish the world struggle from your attitude and your vocabulary.

All that we do now must be done in a sacred manner and in celebration.

We are the ones we've been waiting for.

-The Elders, Oraibi, Arizona Hopi Nation

The Equity Challenge

If "we are the ones we've been waiting for" and "no one else is coming", then what is the work we need to focus on?

We need to focus on the design, development and deployment of engaged learning for all in our schools. In particular, we need to give thought to the experience of learning for:

- First Nations and Métis children whose experience of the system "as is" is often problematic and alienating.

- Those with physical and emotional challenges who are to be "included" yet need more than inclusion – they need to be engaged and empowered.

- Troubled, delinquent and disturbed young people, especially teens, whose sense of identity and purpose is challenged by the monetarist society in which many in Alberta live.

- The sons and daughters of recent immigrants who find adjustment to not just schooling, but society in Alberta difficult and find multiculturalism a challenge.

- Those whose body image and body weight give them cause for anxiety and depression and who experience taunts and bullying.

- The lesbian, transgender, gay young person who is seeking meaning for their statement of sexuality in a society that is getting better at coming to terms with gender identity, but still has a long way to go.

- The exceptional child, whether academically or artistic, for whom schooling seems to be a "drag" on their own felt sense of opportunity.

And for the learner who is already engaged in the learning activities provided by the school. That is, we need to do more than categorize and develop a program; we need to rethink the basis of schooling for all of our learners.

There are a variety of "promises" being made to our communities about schools – promises of quality, relevance and value. But the key promise – that schools would be a place which all would both engage and enjoy the experience of learning – is yet to be made with any conviction. If we are to understand equity as more than "adjustment" and instead see equity as the grand challenge for our school system, then we need to see schools as able to broker the relationship between each learner, knowledge, teacher and community in a way that enlivens and engages.

References

Alberta Council of Women's Shelters. 2013. Alberta Provincial Data Released Oct. 2. https://www.acws.ca/alberta-provincial-shelter-data-released

Government of Canada. 2010. Memorandum of Understanding for First Nations Education in Alberta. Available at http://education.alberta

McCain, M.N., J.F. Mustard and K. McCuaig. 2011. *Early Years Study 3: Making Decisions, Taking Action.* Toronto, ON: Margaret & Wallace McCain Family Foundation.

Schweinhart, L., and D. Weikart. 1993. Success by Empowerment: The High/Scope Perry Preschool Study Through Age 27. Young Children 49, no 1: 54–58.